D0537954

This is much more than a 'cookbook', this is a book about food, people, politics and pleasure. The introduction is an informative well-researched piece of work that taught me more about genetically-modified foods than any government ever did.

I think that what the author Troth Wells and the *New Internationalist* are doing by publishing this high quality, internationalist vegetarian cookery book is great, even revolutionary, and as a passionate vegan it is uplifting for me to see that it contains so many vegan recipes. I like hanging out with the kind of people that cook this stuff.

Dr Benjamin Zephaniah, poet and musician

LONDON BOROUGH OF HACKNEY
3 8040 01301 2010

Vegetarian quick & easy

Cooking from around the world

by Troth Wells

LONDON BOROUGH OF
HACKNEY
LIBRARY SERVICES
LOCAT
HBS
No. VOLS
ACC No.
07/701

Front cover photo by *Mark Mason*.

Quick & Easy vegetarian dishes from around the world for Western kitchens.
First published in the UK by
New Internationalist Publications Ltd
Oxford, England.

Copyright (c) Troth Wells/New Internationalist 2000
and individuals contributing recipes. All rights reserved.

Paperback edition 2001
Reprinted 2005, 2006

Copyright (c) for photographs rests with the individual photographers/agencies.

The book is sold subject to the condition that it shall not, by way of trade or otherwise, be lent, re-sold, hired out or otherwise circulated without the publisher's prior consent in any form of binding or cover other than that in which it is published and without a similar condition including this condition being imposed on the subsequent publisher.

Design by the New Internationalist.

Printed in China by C&C Offset Printing Co. Ltd., China

British Library Cataloguing-in-Publication Data.
A catalogue record for this book is available from the British Library.

New Internationalist Publications Ltd
Registered Office:
55 Rectory Road, Oxford OX4 1BW
United Kingdom.

Foreword

This **Quick & Easy** collection of vegetarian recipes from around the world is the fourth in the New Internationalist food book series, following the **NI Food Book** (1990), **The World in Your Kitchen** (1993), and **The Spices of Life** (1996). These books have been translated and published in the Netherlands, Switzerland, Denmark and Belgium as well as sold in Canada and the US, Australia and Aotearoa/New Zealand.

Readers often comment to me that one of the things they particularly like about these books, in addition to the recipes themselves, is the emphasis on *people* in the many color photos. This emphasis certainly makes the NI books distinctive and it is a deliberate attempt to give a positive view of the women, men and children who all too often appear on our TV screens or in newspapers only as victims.

For wherever we live, whether in Australia or Africa, food is central. We can learn a lot about ingredients and cooking from other regions and one of the most rewarding aspects of producing these books is that they can stimulate discussion on a wide range of topics, as well as stimulating the taste buds.

Troth Wells
New Internationalist
Oxford

Acknowledgements

Special thanks to all the people who sent in recipes for this book, especially Lakshmi Menon, Gowri Rajendran, Pippa Pearce, Dig Woodvine, Andrew Pinney, Seona Smiles, Sarah Byham, Gilly Wright, and Jaba Banerjee. I'd also like to thank Dinyar Godrej for his contribution of recipes, testing, and helpful editing; William Beinart and Michael York for testing recipes; my colleagues at the NI, especially Ian Nixon who designed the book; and my family, whose support is always valued.

Market garden beside Lake Atitlan, Guatemala. PHOTO: JOHN HATT / HUTCHISON

Contents

Future food

As the twenty-first century dawns, we find ourselves facing new frontiers in food production. *Troth Wells* looks at some of the issues that are causing the most concern, starting back in time in the medieval city of Fès, Morocco.

I had been warned. The harsh cry *Balek!* - watch out! - came raking through the air seconds before the donkey lurched into me, its basketwork panniers of ordure giving off an altogether overripe aroma. I squeezed flat against the walls of the choked and narrow street to let the garbage-collection continue, for this was the medieval medina of Fès in Morocco where no cars are allowed and donkeys, mules and their drivers definitely have the right of way. Unimpressed by my alacrity, Alain the guide gently suggested I took myself out of the way for a while by going to look at a *souk* - market - set off the main street. I had explained that I wanted to see food not carpets, and after a meaningful shrugging of shoulders at the weirdness of some tourists, he took to the task with dedication. In a few hours we had walked most of the way around the medina seeing spice sellers, bean and grain markets, damp green mounds of fresh mint sprigs for tea, and tiny stalls selling pastries, sweets or dried fruit. On one corner a vendor spooned hot chickpeas into pockets of delicious *khobz* (bread). A perfect fast-food snack, nutritious and vegetarian. Just what I was looking for in Morocco, quick and easy vegetarian food.

But wait a moment. Don't beans have to soak first, and then cook for hours? Well yes... and no. You can soak and boil them, like other beans and pulses, and in Morocco this is the way they are usually prepared. But there are other ways - as I have been finding out for this book.

The aim of this collection is to provide tasty recipes that are simple to prepare and cook, drawing on dishes found in Africa, Asia, the Caribbean and Latin America, as well as the Middle East. Lots of them use fresh ingredients which do not require long cooking; others use canned or frozen goods, but all of them have been prepared without the shortcuts offered by a microwave or a pressure cooker.

The idea arose from the success of the *New Internationalist*'s earlier vegetarian cookbook, *The World in Your Kitchen*, published in 1993, and the ever-increasing growth of interest in vegetarian food.

There are many reasons for this. Many people do not eat meat for ethical or religious reasons, feeling that animals are equal beings which should not be killed to satisfy human appetites. Some make a distinction between killing animals for food out of necessity, such as in hunter-gatherer societies (although it is the gathering rather than the hunting that provides most of the nutrition). Many dislike the way animals are farmed commercially as production-line units - scrawny chickens cooped in tiny cages; frail veal calves that never see the light of day; beef cattle pumped up on growth hormones and so on. Environmental concerns are also important. Producing animals for human consumption on a vast scale requires vast amounts of animal fodder. Nearly 40 per cent of the world's grain is fed to livestock, but in the US the figure rises to 70 per cent. The world's cattle alone are estimated to chew their way through enough food to provide the calories for 8.7 billion people - well over today's 6 billion global population. And at the other end, as it were, cattle produce waste on a massive scale, and account for 20 per cent of global methane emissions.[1]

Health is another reason why people avoid meat. Well-planned vegetarian diets 'are healthful... nutritionally adequate, and provide health benefits in the prevention of certain diseases', notes the American Dietetic Association, citing lower incidence of heart conditions, high blood pressure and some cancers. Like meat-eaters though, vegetarians can easily eat too

The kasbah souk, Marrakech, Morocco.
PHOTO: JEREMY HORNER / HUTCHISON

much fat - especially if they enjoy dairy produce and some classic veggie standbys like pizza.

Food to suit you

So finding your way into the kinds of food that suit you and your outlook on life can take time and require changes. For instance, one reason people sometimes give for sticking to meat is that it is quick, fuss-free and they know how to cook it. Here's a common enough scene: the kids are clamoring; you are tired; they had baked beans yesterday, and that's the only veggie food they will eat apart from pizza and there isn't any of that. However there is a pack of burgers... and you don't want a battle right now, you have to go out to a meeting that's about to start... and it doesn't seem the moment to try something new...

But on a day with a little more time to think, you might like to try some recipes from this book. They take from 10-40 minutes - start to finish - and many take much less time. This is vital, as we are all spending less time making meals than we used to.

People everywhere, especially women who do most of the world's cooking, are looking for ways to save time. Women in India who can spend hours each day grinding spices may be delighted to find a ready-ground masala - even though of course they know their own is best. And women in Africa heave a sigh of relief if they can afford to buy ground sorghum or maize and put away their pounding stick.

Short cuts

In the West, too, people look to shave minutes off the time they take to prepare food, even though few of us have ever had to grind spices or pound grain for lunch. A National Opinion Poll survey in the UK showed that in the 1980s people spent on average one hour a day preparing food. A decade later, this has dropped to 30 minutes and it is forecast that by the next century we will only spend 11 minutes each day on the task. A poll of 1,000 adults in London showed that 97 per cent took short cuts, using chilled convenience foods, and two thirds said they bought supermarket foods such as pizzas, ready meals and pasta sauces at least once or several times a week. In the US - where else - new kitchenless apartments are apparently being built because people eat out so often. For those who still have a kitchen, some want to feel that they have done more than simply put a ready-made meal into the pan or microwave. The supermarket answer is to produce gourmet meals in kit form - no washing and chopping needed - but you have a sense of making the meal yourself as you cook and mix the ingredients according to the instructions, to produce 'amazing risotto cakes with walnut and tarragon dressing'.

For many vegetarians, ready-meals are a godsend in the busy round of work, kids and home life. But some have a niggling feeling that, tasty as it is, supermarket pizza or mushroom curry is perhaps not a million miles from being junk food, smothered with additives and preservatives.

Do you really want to read the label?

And now of course there is another reason to leave these items out of your shopping basket. Over 60 per cent of our processed food contains soy or maize/corn products - in breakfast cereals, ready-meals, chocolate - but also in vegetarian mainstays like tofu and veggie-burgers.[2] And, as most people are now aware, much of that soy and maize/corn is genetically modified (see box p 12).

It is ironic that soybeans are in the frontline, for soy provides a major source of vegetarian protein - even though most of the world's harvest is used to feed animals. It is doubly ironic that versatile protein-packed soybeans and wholesome golden sweetcorn are now at the cutting edge of agribusiness with millions of dollars and hectares of land caught up in what may be the most dangerous experiment yet. Genetically-modified (GM) crops are already widespread. Globally, nearly 28 million hectares were planted with transgenic (containing genes from another species) crops in 1998 - almost treble the 1997 area.[3] The US is in the vanguard, with over 20 million hectares, followed by China, Argentina, Canada and Australia; and now Mexico and South Africa are also turning over land to the new plants. A feverish debate has arisen over the ethics as well as the economics of the practice of gene manipulation itself, the way the technology is being used, and the impact on people all around the world, including Morocco.

Street life

Skalli's pavement cafe in Fès seemed a long way from the cut and thrust of global agribusiness, but it was a good place to think about food as well as eating it. The little cafe with its tables and chairs spilling out onto the street is right next to the

Donkeys and oranges - memorable features of Morocco's medinas.

market which, early in the day, is full of color and bustle. Today's prices are chalked up on a huge board at the market entrance, and the stalls groan with an abundance of gleaming fruit, vegetables, dates and olives. Morocco's beneficent climate enables the country to steal a march on European producers: its tomatoes, potatoes and oranges are prized for their taste and quality. What pleasure to wander among the stalls, buying a few grapes before strolling along to the cafe for breakfast. Behind his counter of date pastries, *m'hancha* - the cinnamon-dusted 'snake' cake - and other delights, Skalli invites me to try little almond crescents with sesame seeds. So I sit, coffee and cakes at hand, idly flicking through the local French-language newspaper.

There's a report on agriculture that catches my eye: it's a pie-chart about genetically-engineered crops. And I had thought I was safe in Morocco. But of course the whole world can be affected by this pioneering technology, and many countries have been importing GM crops (often unwittingly) for years. Morocco itself imports soybeans from the US, and since well over half the US soy crop is GM, chances are that Morocco's imported soy is too.[4]

What are GM crops?

Genetically modified plants and seeds are those whose genetic make-up has been altered to achieve some desired characteristic (see box opposite). Take a field of soybeans growing in Iowa. The young plants poke up through the earth and begin to spread their leaves and grow. But alongside them the weeds flourish in the rich, well-cared for soil. What does the farmer do? Break out the herbicide and spray the field... but then the soybeans would perish too. So the scientists set to work to change the genetic pattern of the soybean seeds by introducing a gene that can tolerate the herbicide, and - hey presto! - the soybeans flourish under a mist of heavy chemicals, while the weeds weaken and perish. All seems well, but then the insects move in and chomp their way into the soybeans. In the lab another gene is added: this time from the common soil bacterium, *bacillus thuringiensis* (Bt), which is a natural pesticide zapping a range of common insects. So now the soybeans, brand name Roundup Ready, can stand proud and unblemished. It seems to be a triumph of technology, human ingenuity, and (lest we forget) big business.

But when the weeds die, so do the animals and insects that feed on them. And in time, the weeds develop resistance and become stronger, requiring new techniques to quell them. The same is true of the Bt bacterium which, ironically, has long been used by organic farmers as a natural pesticide; they fear that its overuse in GM crops will lead to a new generation of superpests.

There are many issues wrapped up in the biotech debate - from the environment, as seen above, to health, corporate dominance, food security, and even democracy. These concerns are set to have an even greater impact as more fields are planted.

Cut and paste genes

A quick guide to genetic engineering

Imagine you're a genetic engineer and your company has told you that it needs **a tobacco plant that glows in the dark**. Nothing else will do.

So you take a glow-worm and you find out which part of its DNA code 'tells' it to glow - a process known as *gene mapping* or *gene sequencing*.

Then you get hold of some *enzymes* (chemicals) - different ones will cut the DNA strand in different places. By using the right ones, you can lift out the *genes* for glowing.

The same trick will cut open the DNA of the tobacco plant at a suitable point, making a 'gap' into which the glow fragment can be inserted and 'glued' into place by more enzymes.

The small fragment of glow-worm DNA has now been spliced into the much larger DNA of the tobacco plant - *Recombinant DNA*.

Put this back into a cell and it will eventually produce ... **a tobacco plant that glows in the dark**.

PJ Polyp

You may become what you eat

Health concerns are widespread, focusing on two major anxieties: one is that we could become resistant to an important antibiotic, while the second is that we may already be eating more GM foods than we realise.

The box on page 11 tries to explain how genetic engineering works. When a new gene is introduced into a cell, it is often linked to a 'marker' gene so that the desired gene can be easily identified. A favorite marker gene for this purpose is an ampicillin (antibiotic)-resistant one. When GM maize, such as Novartis Bt, with its ampicillin-resistant gene enters the food chain, the bacteria in human and animal guts could become resistant to this key antibiotic, and render it useless.

It could be you - it almost certainly is!

Consumers are edgy about health too because they may not know what they are eating. Food labelling will not necessarily help them. For example, in the European Union, only 10-15 per cent of products containing GM soy will be labelled as such, even though some 60 per cent of processed food contains it. Retailers are not obliged to label the rest - the majority of such foods - because the soy oil or additive lecithin do not contain 'detectable' quantities of GM material (see box). But that genetically-engineered material is still present, whatever the quantities. As one of the UK's largest supermarkets, Tesco, noted when explaining why the store could not become GM free: 'some foods derived from a genetically modified source, ie oil and lecithin, may contain genetically modified traces'.[5]

This is quite a revelation. Although as yet there is little hard evidence that eating GM foods damages us in any way, there was a case in the US in 1989 where 37 people died, 1,500 were permanently disabled and 5,000 people became ill after consuming a dietary supplement *L-tryptophan*, made by a Japanese company that had recently introduced a new GM-bacterium into its production process.[6]

Alarm bells

So far no-one knows for sure what the long-term consequences of eating GM food will be. The advocates foresee no major problems, the rest are more sceptical - perhaps especially in Europe where memories linger of the way BSE (mad cow disease) was handled, and government assurances were found to be incorrect. Once bitten, twice shy. 'If BSE has taught us anything,' commented *The Good Food Guide*, 'It is surely to be cautious about tampering with natural process, however well intentioned, however plausibly the benefits are packaged.'

The artificial nature of genetically engineering plants or animals does not automatically make it dangerous. But the process is a major departure from traditional breeding techniques in that it is possible to cross the natural boundaries between species. As seen earlier, Monsanto's Roundup Ready soybeans contain a soil bacterium gene which makes them resistant to insect pests. In a further leap, anti-freeze genes from arctic fish have been introduced into tomatoes and potatoes to try and make these frost-resistant.

Currently, most GM ingredients are in processed foods, so to eat less GM material, eat as few processed foods as possible.

- Many scientists are concerned about the safety of these foods which can contain foreign genes from bacteria, viruses, fish and animals.
- Most processed foods contain GM soya or maize.
- Fresh fruit and vegetables in the US and Canada may be genetically modified.
- There are currently no GM fresh fruit and vegetables on sale in the UK.
- GM soya from the US is an ingredient in around 60 per cent of processed foods including bread, biscuits, baby milk, baby foods, breakfast cereals, margarine, soups, pasta, pizza, ready meals, flour, sweets, ice-cream, crisps, chocolate, soy sauce, veggie-burgers, tofu, soya milk (it is also used in meat products).
- GM maize/corn from the US can be present in processed ready meals, soups, sauces, curry sauces, cake mixes, crisps, snacks and chewing gum.
- Many additives from GM micro-organisms are approved for sale, and currently these do **not** have to be labelled in Europe. Examples are riboflavin (vitamin B^2) as E101 and E101A, soya oil and lecithin (E322) from GM soya which are widely used in processed foods.
- Where possible buy organic foods or those which are guaranteed free from GM ingredients. If unsure, avoid soya-based ingredients like soya flour, soya oil, vegetable oil, lecithin and hydrolysed vegetable protein; and maize-based ingredients like modified starch, cornflour, corn oil, corn syrup, dextrose, glucose and polenta.

Source: Peter Brown *Avoid GM Foods*
http://wkweb4.cableinet.co.uk/pbrown/avoidgm/gmfoods.htm

The anxiety centres on the unpredictability of the new organisms: we do not know yet what their long-term impacts will be. But some GM crops have already leapt the fence and cross-pollinated with wild plants. 'Scientists have discovered the first genetically-modified superweeds in Britain,' reported the *Independent on Sunday*, after pollen from a GM trial crop spread to wild turnip plants.[7] The Government's official wildlife advisor, English Nature, said this discovery 'proves its predictions that planting GM crops will lead to the creation of new hybrids'. So with all the uncertainty that surrounds these plants, how did they get this far? The answer lies in the corporate world.

Biotech behemoths

The medina in Fès seems steeped in other-worldliness, with its ancient mosques and *medersas* (religious colleges). Sipping mint tea after a plateful of grilled aubergine with olives, bread and the fiery local sauce, *harissa*, I watch people walking by. Men wearing medieval monk-like caftans with pointed hoods stroll towards the nearby mosque. The lack of motor vehicles adds to the sense that we are in a different world. But if I lift up my eyes to the tops of houses I can see white TV satellite dishes all around, and I know that the global advertising messages will be beaming down.

Just at that moment a donkey comes clattering around the corner; this one is laden with red crates which look familiar. Yes, it's Coca Cola - the logo looks very fetching in Arabic script. How do they do it? Everywhere you go, there it is. That fizzy drink is a testimony to global reach and corporate strength, a power that is shared by the agribusiness companies. Ten corporations control 85 per cent of the world's agrochemical market, valued at around $31 billion. The top five vegetable seed companies control three-quarters of the global vegetable seed market.[8] And several of these corporations are pioneering GM crops. The names Monsanto, Aventis and Novartis crop up time and again. In the US, Monsanto's genetically-engineered seeds made up 88 per cent of the transgenic crop area in 1998.[9]

TROTH WELLS / NEW INTERNATIONALIST

Reach for the sky - despite its medieval feel, the old city of Fès is tuned in to the global economy.

Consumer choice - customers size up the produce in Place Saffarine, Fès.

JEREMY HORNER / HUTCHISON

And the biotech business does not stop at plants. In a landmark ruling, the US Supreme Court granted a patent to General Electric for a GM bacterium that could digest oil. The Court ruled that the 'relevant distinction is not between animate and inanimate things but whether living products could be seen as "human-made" inventions'. This 1980 decision opened the floodgates for patent applications on plants, seeds, animals, human tissue and genes, mostly from Northern companies. The knock-on effect was felt in Europe too, where a Life Patents Directive was passed in May 1998, allowing for the patenting of life forms.

The agrochemical companies have been using patented organisms to improve and extend their range of products. 'Plant protection' - herbicides and pesticides to you and me - forms a large part of their operations. But as the effects of agrochemicals on humans and animals became apparent with pollution and poisoning, especially in the Majority World where there was less safety regulation, the companies responded by trying to cut out the need to dose plants with chemicals. Their solution was to try and incorporate the characteristics of the herbicide or pesticide within the plant's own genetic material, so producing a better crop to grow more food. 'Anything that improves the taste, availability and variety of produce for the US consumer should have an overall positive impact on the citizens of the world's health and wealth,' announced David Evans of DNA Plant Technology in California.[10] It sounds altruistic enough, but critics point out that profit rather than humanitarian concern was, and is, the main motive. Two of the main anti-GM campaigners, the Rural Advancement Foundation International (RAFI) in Canada and Genetic Resources Action International (GRAIN) based in Spain, assert that breeding the characteristics that relate to sustainability and feeding the world are far off the corporate agenda.

'Food, Health, Hope'

Monsanto's public image on this theme has drawn an angry response. In a forceful publicity campaign their advertisements trumpeted 'Let the harvest begin' and then, in the eyes of many, went on to give a totally distorted picture of the potential of GM crops to feed developing countries. Reporters on India's *Down to Earth* environmental magazine called the adverts 'a riot' and said Monsanto had been 'leaning over backwards to project itself as a company with philanthropic intentions "to feed the world"'. A group of delegates from 22 African countries (including Morocco) at the UN's Food and Agriculture Organization (FAO) in Rome took particular exception to the way 'the image of the poor and hungry from our countries is being used by giant multinational corporations to push a technology that is neither safe, environmentally friendly, nor economically beneficial to us.' Thus they gave the lie to Monsanto's syrupy strapline 'Food, Health, Hope'.

There is already enough food in the world for each person; the FAO states that per capita 'dietary energy supply' increased by 11 per cent during the 21-year period between 1969-71 and 1990-1, from 2,440 calories a day to 2,720.[11] The optimal requirement level is 2,600 calories per day. Bluster about producing more food to feed the world is a diversion, for as usual the problem is not with supply but distribution and people's ability to pay. 'Food has always been about power and money,' says Harriet Friedman of the University of Toronto. It's a view shared by physicist and environmental campaigner Vandana Shiva: 'Far from feeding the world, people are going to starve *because* of genetically-engineered foods. More and more peasants will see their crops substituted though biotechnology.' She adds that trials of GM crops, currently going on in many countries around the world, show that genetic engineering is not coming into agriculture through the freedom of choice of producers and consumers. 'It is being sneaked in by stealth,' says Shiva, who believes that the companies' rush to push GM seeds into the fields is threatening democracy and freedom in fundamental ways.[12]

CRISPIN HUGHES / HUTCHISON

In the wind - GM seeds may threaten food security in the Majority World.

Under wraps

As we have seen, consumers may have no idea that the foods they are eating already contain GM foods or organisms, as labelling where it exists is patchy. Many of the field trials have been carried out in a secretive manner. But the anti-democratic charge made by Shiva and many others goes deeper than this. For not only are farmers encouraged to use unproven technology and consumers expected to eat test-tube foods, there is a new nasty on the horizon, dubbed The Terminator by RAFI. This is the seed that is genetically engineered so that it cannot reproduce - it is a 'suicide seed'. This new seed is seen as a threat to agricultural biodiversity and to the food security of the 1.4 billion rural people who rely on seed they save each year to plant the following season.[13] When The Terminator strikes - and two top companies in this field (Monsanto and AstraZeneca) have already applied for patents in 89 and 77 countries respectively - the age-old practice of saving seeds to use again, and of exchanging them with neighbors could be outlawed.[14]

Why, one wonders, would any canny farmer co-operate? The answer is that she or he does not have any choice. The large companies have tightened their grip on the vegetable seed market, so every time farmers need new stock - as they must have from time to time, in addition to saving their own - they find themselves propelled into the arms of agribusiness. The companies work hard to nurture their clients, including government agencies, binding them closer and closer with promises of wonderful harvests from miracle seeds that will thrive as long as the farmer uses a particular fertilizer, herbicide or pesticide which just happens to be manufactured by the same company. There is little option to buy elsewhere - just five companies control virtually all of this seed market. The Terminator technique is to activate or de-activate the ability of such seeds to germinate, and farmers will have to pay a royalty in order to receive the chemicals needed to kick-start the seeds into life.

Companies that can render seeds sterile know that this safeguards all the genetic tinkering they have done or will do. Firstly, the seed has been patented, and secondly the designer genes it carries are locked securely because the seeds can only be reactivated on application and payment of royalties. This sounds like fairly watertight protection for the already-powerful biotech companies, but in case they need more help, the World Trade Organization (WTO) can help, as happened with the US vs India.

Tripping India

With the setting up of the WTO in 1994 and its familiar, the Trade-Related Intellectual Property Rights (TRIPS), no farmers are safe from the tentacles of globalization. For example, when India tried to avoid importing soybeans from the US, saying that, thanks, it already had plenty of soybeans of its own, the US got heavy and pointed out that under the WTO rules no member state can refuse another's goods except on safety grounds. India finally agreed to import one million tonnes. 'Farmers in the US [were] expecting to plant twice as much GM Soya in 1998 as in 1997,' says Oxfam 'And with resistance to GM Soya in Europe there are concerns that it will be dumped in countries like India [and depress prices]'.[15]

Another organization campaigning on the issue, Christian Aid, points out that although consumers in the West can try to reject and/or regulate GM products, these crops are increasingly being grown in Majority World countries and will come back as imports. As often happens, countries in the South are caught in the iron grip of Western commercial interests. Biotech companies are seeking patents on lab versions of crops on which poor countries rely such as rice, quinoa, coconut and palm kernel oil. And Majority World people could well have GM crops like maize or tomatoes foisted upon them without proper debate.

Lying low - greenhouses on Morocco's coast. Morocco is one of many countries where GM crops have been tested.

TROTH WELLS / NEW INTERNATIONALIST

Greenhouse genes

I'm travelling along Morocco's coast. The sea rolls onto the shore, spraying surf onto the golden sand - the kind of perfection conjured by a million tourist brochures. Between me and that tempting spot lie sloping verdant fields, soaking up sunshine, many covered with plastic greenhouses. Now and again I could glimpse the plants inside. They were tomatoes, one of Morocco's major crops with about one million tonnes produced each year.

But the problem with tomatoes is that they go soft too quickly, especially if you are a multinational company that wants to harvest them in Kenya and sell them in Australia. Monsanto's solution to this is 'FlavrSavr' tomatoes. The glib ad agency name shows a lack of taste and so apparently do the tomatoes themselves.

FlavrSavr have been grown in Guatemala - even though it has hundreds of indigenous varieties - without the consent of the authorities.[16] Although the tomatoes were grown in greenhouses, there is no way as yet of knowing whether the transgenic tomatoes have spread beyond.

It is at this moment that I recall that field tests on genetically engineered crops have also been carried out in Morocco.[17] Am I looking at transgenic tomatoes? Suddenly, looking again at those ranks of greenhouses, I feel a science-fiction shiver down my spine... tomato triffids?

We are certainly on the edge of a brave new world, a world where traditional agriculture will bear the brunt of technological changes. And while everyone recognizes that things cannot stand still, traditional farming can always be improved - for example with the development of more local seeds. The shockwaves of the biotech business will destabilize and possibly destroy already fragile economies. Back in 1997, US farmers suffered when a crop of Monsanto's Bollgard cotton failed, and of course they were wealthy by comparison with Majority World farmers. It is surely unwise to increase our dependence on GM seeds for food crops which could also fail us, and may have long-term effects on animals and humans. According to the FAO the world depends on too few crops, and 'replacement of local varieties' is the main cause.

On a plate

While thinking about this, and about fast-foods, ready meals and so on, I am confronted with a sheep's head on a plate, knife and fork in readiness at the side. In fact there is a whole row of them. It is dusk in Marrakech, and I am strolling around the vast *Djemma el Fna* square in the heart of the city, vaguely looking for supper. There are food stalls all around lit by lanterns, with benches to sit on, and eager cooks vying with each other as they call for trade. Even though I decline the offer of sheep's head, it is clear that lots of other people rate it highly - the stall soon fills up. I wander back to the hotel and settle for the fixed-price menu, sad to see that it contains mostly French rather than Moroccan food.

At one corner of the Moorish-style dining room the waiters are preparing a buffet feast or *diffa* for the upmarket guests. First a tureen of *harira*, Morocco's famous bean soup, is brought to the table. Large earthenware *tagines* of stew are given pride of place as the centerpiece along with pale mounds of *couscous* or semolina. Next come plates laden with cooked vegetables and grilled aubergines; round dishes containing green lentils and haricot beans in tomato sauce; potatoes cooked with saffron and pickled lemons; red onions cooked with raisins and honey...

I call the waiter. Would it be possible, I suggest, for me to have just one of the vegetarian dishes from the buffet instead of the set menu? He looks at me, thoughtful. 'You mean you don't want the lamb *tagine* or the beef cooked with olives?' I shake my head.

'Well, in that case there's no problem - you can have what you like at no extra cost!'

I needed no second bidding. Eating vegetarian has its advantages.

There was a wealth of new things to try that night and one or two of the dishes have been included in this book. Other recipes have been sent in - all of them are quick to cook - and I hope you'll enjoy the diversity of ingredients, aromas and tastes.

1 Chris Dessent, 'Cooking up a Revolution' from The Vegetarian Summer 1998, The Vegetarian Society. **2** Genetically engineered food, The Vegetarian Society information sheet 1999. **3** Clive James, 1998 in Rafi Communique Jan/Feb 1999. **4** Selling Suicide: Farming, false promises and genetic modification in the developing world, Christian Aid Briefing Paper 10 May 1999. **5** Letter from Tesco Customer Services dated 5 May 1999. **6** *The New Internationalist*, No 293 August 1997. **7** *The Independent on Sunday* 18 April 1999. **8** Lynn Grooms 'With merger completed, Harris Moran Focuses on Future' in *Seeds and Crop Digest* January 1999, quoted in Rafi Communique March/April 1999. **9** Rafi Communique March/April 1999. **10** Ricarda Steinbrecher, 'From Green to Gene Revolution', *The Ecologist* Vol 26 No 6 Nov/Dec 1996 quoted in *The New Internationalist* No 293 August 1997 p 8. **11** The Sixth World Food Survey 1997 edition, FAO, Rome. **12** Vandana Shiva, 'Uprooting the seeds of hope', Guardian Unlimited Archive, 31 March 1999. http://www.guardianunlimited.co.uk **13** Traitor Technology, Rafi Communique January/February 1999. **14** Traitor Technology: ' "Damaged goods" from the Gene Giants' RAFI News Release 29 March 1999. **15** Laura Spinney, 'Biotechnology in Crops: issues for the developing world', Oxfam Research paper, May 1998. **16** Biotechnology in Crops, Oxfam 1998. **17** *The New Internationalist* No 293 August 1997, p 19.

DEXTER TIRANTI

Remains of the day - at dusk people throng the foodstalls of the *Djemma el Fna* square in Marrakech.

Ingredients Gallery

Here are some items which are handy to have around, although they are not all required for the recipes contained in this book. See also the **Glossary**, p 167.

Chilli and chilli powder

Cardamom

Coriander/ cilantro

(clockwise from top) Walnut, pine nuts, almond, cashew, pistachio, hazel

Black peppercorns

White peppercorns

Papaya/ pawpaw

Turmeric
Onion seeds
Poppy seeds
Mustard seeds
Sweet red pepper (pimiento)
Galangal
Bak choi (Chinese cabbage)
Mung bean sprouts

Cinnamon
Avocado
pear
Soy
sauce
Red kidney
beans
Maize/
corn
Sesame
seeds/
Tahina
Chickpeas/
garbanzos
Coconut
milk
Nutmeg
and
Mace
Lemon
grass
LIGHT SUPERIOR SOY SAUCE
150ml
JEFI
COCONUT MILK
LAIT DE COCO
KOKOSMILCH
PREMIUM
QUALITY
NET. 400 ml (14 FL. OZ.)

Mushrooms
Cumin
Couscous
Paprika
Ras el
Hanout
Wakame
seaweed
Red lentils, Basmati
rice & Cloves
Saffron
Ginger

Nutrition Guide

Shop selling curd, Sri Lanka.

PHOTO: DOMINIC SANSONI / IMPACT

Nutrition Guide

Vegetarians in the West generally have a rich basket of foods to choose from, and run small risk of missing vital nutrients. This basic guide takes you through what your body needs and how to get it from non-meat foods. If you base your meals on salads, vegetables and whole cereals with moderate amounts of nuts, pulses, fruit, dried fruit and dairy products (non-vegans) you will obtain all the necessary nutrients.

What humans require

Our bodies need water, carbohydrates, fiber, protein, fat/oil, vitamins and minerals. Carbohydrates, protein and fat are known as macronutrients, measured in grams (g). Equally important, but needed in far smaller amounts are the micronutrients - vitamins, minerals and trace elements - which are measured in milligrams (mg) or micrograms (µg or mcg). In addition to these we need water and fiber.

Regular intakes of nutrients are necessary to maintain our bodies and to give us energy, measured in calories. A person's calorie requirement varies according to their age, health, size and activity level. So a small person with a sedentary life may only require 2,000 calories a day while someone who is large and does heavy physical work may need 3,500. The World Health Organization (WHO) and Food and Agriculture Organization (FAO) recommend a minimum daily intake for adults of 2,600 calories per person, with variations as noted above about size and lifestyle.

To best nourish the body, these calories should be drawn from the range of nutrients listed above. For although you could rapidly get nearly all the calories you need in a day from eating a pack of butter - half a pound (225g) would yield around 2,025 calories - this would leave your body lacking other vital ingredients (and probably make you sick). The main or macro-nutrients - carbohydrates, protein and fat - provide different amounts of calories. Fat, as we have just seen, is very high in calories: one gram of oil, butter or margarine brings with it a hefty nine calories. Carbohydrates (from sugars and starches) and protein (from beans, nuts and dairy foods) both provide four calories for each gram. Alcohol delivers seven calories per gram (or milliliter), so a glass of dry white wine would be about 100 calories.

Protein

Protein is the building material making up part of the structure of every cell in our bodies, and since cells are constantly dying and being replaced we require a steady supply of protein for this rebuilding. Infants and children need plenty as they are growing rapidly.

Proteins are made up of amino acids containing molecules of carbon, hydrogen, nitrogen, oxygen and sulphur. There are around 20 amino acids altogether and all life forms have them. Humans can manufacture some amino acids from other foods, but there are eight (nine for children) which must be ingested. These are the 'essential' amino acids - valine, leucine, isoleucine, lysine, threonine, tryptophan, methionine, phenylalanine (and histadine for children).

Foods contain amino acids in differing proportions. The highest-quality protein foods contain the most complete set of essential amino acids in the right proportions for the body to be able to make the best use of them. According to the American Dietetic Association, 'plant sources of protein alone can provide adequate amounts of essential amino acids if a variety of plant foods are consumed and energy needs are met'. And as we mix foods throughout the day, the lack of an amino acid in one can be offset by another: for example, pulses are low in methionine but rich in lysine, while cereals are the other way about.

The Association also points out that these 'complementary' proteins do not need to be consumed at the same time, as long as they are taken over the course of the day. Many traditional diets in the South are made up of these balancing ingredients - beans with corn/maize tortillas in Latin America, for example; lentils and rice in India or hummus (chickpeas and sesame seed paste) with wheat pitta bread in the Middle East. For non-vegans, adding dairy produce and eggs also supplies missing amino acids, and as your body can store them for short periods it is unlikely that you would go short.

The World Health Organization recommends that around 10 per cent of a person's energy intake should be in the form of protein. So on an intake of 2,600 calories (the recommended daily amount for adults) about 260 should be as protein. Since each gram of protein provides four calories, you would therefore need 65g of protein each day, depending on your age, sex, lifestyle and so on. The WHO figure leaves a comfortable margin: the UK Vegetarian Society suggests that 45g per day is plenty for women (more if pregnant, breastfeeding or very active) and 55g for men (more if very active). In the period 1990-92, people in the UK consumed an average 92 grams of protein per day (112g in the US; 101g in Australia; 91g in the Netherlands).

People in the rich world rarely lack protein because overall we consume well above the 2,600 calories level:

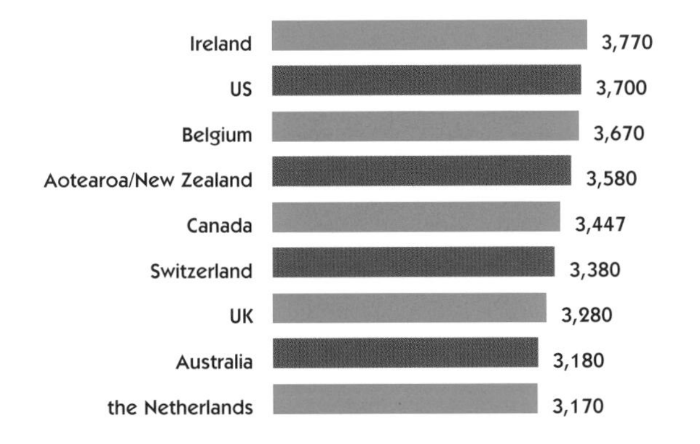

Within that food intake there is likely to be sufficient protein. It is a different situation in countries where the overall calorie consumption is low (the 500 million people of the least developed countries rarely consume more than 2,000 calories; the lowest is Sierra Leone's 1,590).

In the West we have an abundance of protein-rich foods readily available all year round. Vegetarian foods rich in protein include nuts, seeds, pulses (peas, beans, lentils), grains, soy products, dairy produce and eggs. And of course, other foods you eat such as vegetables, salads and fruit contribute small amounts of amino acids as well.

Foods rich in protein

Nuts	hazels, brazils, almonds, cashews, walnuts, pine nuts/pignoles.
Seeds	sesame, pumpkin, sunflower.
Pulses	peas, beans, lentils, peanuts.
Grains/cereals	wheat (in bread, pasta etc), barley, rye, oats, millet, maize/corn/sweetcorn, rice.
Soya products	tofu/beancurd, tempeh, textured vegetable protein, veggie-burgers, soy milk (but be aware that many soy products may now contain **genetically-modified** soy, see **Introduction** p 12).
Dairy products	milk, cheese, yogurt (butter and cream are poor sources of protein), free range eggs.

Carbohydrates

Although protein and fat also provide calories, carbohydrates are our main source of energy. In plant foods, these normally come as sugars and starches.

Where possible, avoid sugars and refined starches, such as white bread or flour and white rice, as although they bring calories, these are 'empty' - meaning they bring few nutrients to the body. On a diet high in refined starches and sugar people quickly become unhealthy because they lack vitamins and minerals. By contrast, cereals such as wholemeal bread, pasta and oats; and root vegetables like potatoes and parsnips bring nourishment to the body for the same amount of calories. They also provide fiber or roughage, the indigestible but essential material which keeps food moving regularly along the gut.

Fats and oils

We all need a little fat to keep body tissues healthy, for the manufacture of hormones and to carry the vitamins A, D, E and K. Fats are made up of smaller components called fatty acids. Two of these, linoleic and linolenic, are essential for humans and they are widely found in plant foods.

There are saturated and unsaturated fats: this refers to how much hydrogen they contain. Saturated fats, found mainly in animal products, contain cholesterol. This is necessary for health but our bodies can produce what they require. But in the West we consume a lot of energy as fat and sugar, often resulting in heart disease and illnesses associated with obesity which kill around 2.5 million people each year. The American Dietetic Association notes that vegetarian diets 'offer disease protection benefits because of their lower saturated fat, cholesterol, and animal protein content'.

Excess cholesterol may build up as deposits on the walls of arteries and clog them, leading to an increased risk of heart disease. Saturated fats raise blood cholesterol levels while unsaturated fats lower them. Mono-unsaturated fats such as olive oil have a neutral effect. Oils which are high in polyunsaturates (and which contain the two essential fatty acids) are safflower, soy bean oil and sunflower oil. Margarines made of these can also be high in polyunsaturated fat. But here the 'catch' is with hydrogenation, the process that turns vegetable oil into margarine. Partially-hydrogenated oils produce 'trans-fats' which cannot be absorbed by the body and can cause cell damage and even heart disease.

But just how much fat should you eat? WHO advises between 15-30 per cent of your total energy intake, with no more than 10 per cent of it in the form of saturated fat. So if your total calorie intake is the recommended level of 2,600 and 20 per cent of this comes from fat, that would be 520 calories. Since each gram of fat brings nine calories, this means you should eat about 58g or two ounces a day. Over the period 1990-1992 people in the North consumed on average nearly 150g / 6 ounces of fat a day: the Danes currently top this poll, each consuming 179g daily, while in Burundi the figure is just 14g per person per day. Remembering that each gram of fat delivers nine calories, the West's daily average intake delivers 1,350 calories before you start adding in the calories from protein and carbohydrates.

Many of the fast foods eaten today, especially by children and heavy adults, contain high amounts of fat. In French fries/chips for example, 50 per cent of the calories are from fat; in a pork sausage, 65 per cent; while in a packet of crisps/chips

Roasting barley, Ladakh, India. PHOTO: DARIUSZ KLEMENS

fat accounts for 60 per cent of the total energy. Meat contributes over 25 per cent of all fat in meat-eaters' diets.

Dairy products are also laden with saturated fat, especially hard cheeses, cream and whole milk - but you are unlikely to polish off half a pound of cheese at one go. There are plenty of dairy products which are low in fat and can deliver the useful protein without the potential for flab. Yogurt, cottage and other low-fat cheeses and skimmed milk are all widely available. Plant foods rich in fats - avocado pears, nuts and seeds - should also be eaten in moderation, ideally in their raw state, and as part of a meal rather than as a snack. However unlike crisps or French fries, nuts and seeds do also provide protein, vitamins and a substantial amount of fiber. Pulses, whole grains, vegetables and fruit are low in fat.

Vitamins and Minerals

In addition to the main or macro-nutrients - protein, carbohydrates and fats - our bodies need vitamins, minerals and trace elements (the micro-nutrients).

VITAMINS

This is the name for a group of unrelated nutrients that the body cannot synthesize for itself either at all or in sufficient quantities. Only small amounts are needed but they must be included in our food. Vitamins are essential for growth, cell repair and regulating metabolism (the rate at which the body consumes energy). Green leafy vegetables are a major source of many vitamins and minerals - try and eat them uncooked where appropriate.

Vitamin A (retinol)

This is essential for healthy eyes and skin and for seeing in dim light. Lack of vitamin A leads to low resistance to infection, skin complaints, fatigue and night blindness. It is found in animal products but our bodies can also manufacture it from carotene which occurs in red and yellow vegetables such as carrots, tomatoes, apricots and bell peppers as well as in green vegetables. It is usually added to margarine.

Some sources of Vitamin A
Broccoli • Carrots • Cheddar • Dandelion leaves • Dried apricots Eggs • Mangoes • Melon • Milk • Parsley • Sorrel • Spinach Sweet potatoes • Watercress

Vitamin B^1 (thiamin)

Thiamin converts carbohydrates into energy and is essential for the growth and health of skin, nerves and muscles. It is easily destroyed through cooking and storage. Deficiency of thiamin leads to poor digestion, skin and hair; and depression and nervous disorders.

Some sources of Vitamin B^1
Bran • Brazil nuts • Hazelnuts • Millet • Oatmeal • Peanuts Peas • Rye flour • Soy flour • Walnuts • Wheatgerm Wholewheat flour/bread • Yeast extract

Vitamin B^2 (riboflavin)

Vitamin B^2 is important for growth and for healthy skin, mouth and eyes. It is destroyed by light. Milk, a main source, can lose up to 70 per cent of B^2 content if it is left in sunlight for two hours. Lack of B^2 shows as bloodshot eyes, mouth sores, dry hair and skin, nervousness and tiredness.

Some sources of Vitamin B^2
Almonds • Brie, Cheddar and other cheeses • Broccoli Broad beans • Dates • Dried peaches • Eggs • Milk Millet • Mushrooms • Soy flour and products Wheatgerm ● Wholewheat bread • Yogurt

Vitamin B^3 (niacin or nicotinic acid)

This is essential for growth, for healthy skin and nerves as well as for the digestion of carbohydrates. Deficiency of this vitamin can result in irritability, nervousness, stomach upsets, headaches and insomnia. Severe lack causes pellagra, a skin disease. The vitamin can be produced in the body from the amino acid tryptophan, found in milk and eggs.

Some sources of Vitamin B^3
Bran • Broad beans • Dates • Dried apricots • Dried peaches Millet • Mushrooms • Peanuts • Soy flour • Wholewheat flour/bread • Yeast extract

Vitamin B^6 (pyridoxine)

B^6 is essential for the body's use of protein; for healthy skin, nerves and muscles. It is particularly important for women who are pregnant, who use the contraceptive pill, or who suffer from pre-menstrual tension. High alcohol consumption increases the body's need for this vitamin, and it is most effective in conjunction with vitamin B^2 and magnesium. B^6 is easily destroyed by cooking. Lack of it brings irritability, depression, skin complaints, insomnia, fatigue, anemia and migraine.

Some sources of Vitamin B^6
Avocado pear • Bananas • Bran • Brie and other cheeses Brussels sprouts • Cauliflower • Currants, sultanas • Hazelnuts • Milk Peanuts • Prunes • Rye flour • Soy flour • Walnuts • Wheatgerm Wholewheat flour/bread • Yeast extract

Vitamin B^{12} (cobalmins or cyanocobalamin)

This is required for growth and for the body's use of protein as well as for the health of nerves and skin. It is easily destroyed by light and heat. Deficiency leads to anemia, tiredness, skin disorders and in extreme cases, paralysis. B^{12} is mainly found in animal products and if you are a vegan you need to take a supplement of this vitamin or eat products which have been fortified with it.

Some sources of Vitamin B^{12}
Cheese • Cottage cheese • Cream • Eggs • Milk Yeast extract • Yogurt

Folic acid (B group)

Folic acid is vital for growth, fertility and healthy blood. As its name suggests, it is found in leafy vegetables. The vitamin is easily lost in cooking so eat plenty of raw salad leaves. In particular, pregnant women and those taking oral contraceptives need folic acid. Deficiency results in anemia, depression, diarrhea, and fetal neural tube defects.

Some sources of Folic acid
Almonds • Avocado pear • Bran • Broccoli Cabbage • Hazelnuts • Parsley • Peanuts Peas • Spinach • Sweet potatoes • Yeast extract

Biotin and pantothenic acid (B group)

Biotin is essential for good skin, nerves and muscles and its lack can lead to hair loss and eczema. Pantothenic acid promotes hair and other tissue growth, and deficiency gives dry skin and hair. These vitamins are found in eggs, yeast, wheatgerm, nuts, wholemeal bread and brown rice.

Vitamin C (ascorbic acid)

This maintains connective tissue between cells; it is needed to maintain healthy teeth and gums; for proper absorption of iron (best eaten at the same meal); it helps prevent disease and assists recovery. Larger amounts are needed by people under stress or taking drugs including antibiotics, tranquillizers, alcohol, nicotine and coffee. Vitamin C is destroyed by cooking and heat. To avoid deficiency, eat plenty of raw fruit and vegetables, and only lightly cook the rest. Deficiency leads to weakening of connective tissue and bleeding (of gums), as well as low resistance to infection.

Some sources of Vitamin C
Bell peppers, red and green • Blackcurrants • Broccoli • Cabbage Grapefruit • Lemons • Lychees • Mangoes • Oranges • Parsley Radishes • Raspberries • Sorrel • Spinach • Strawberries • Watercress

Vitamin D (calciferol)

This is required for the absorption of calcium and phosphorus, and in the formation of bones and teeth. It is formed by the action of sunlight on oils in the skin and it is also available in dairy and other foods. Lack of vitamin D can lead to rickets, and to weakened or porous bones.

Some sources of Vitamin D
Butter • Cheese • Eggs • Margarine • Sunlight

Vitamin E (tocopherol)

This is needed for body cell formation and maintenance and possibly for fertility. It also helps wounds heal without scarring and may have a rejuvenating effect. It is rare to have a deficiency of this vitamin, but it causes tiredness and anemia. Vitamin E is available in most foods.

Vitamin K

Vitamin K is essential for blood-clotting. Lack of it leads to prolonged bleeding, but deficiency is rare since it occurs widely in vegetables and cereals.

Minerals

These are required, like vitamins, to keep the body functioning properly. Calcium, iron, potassium and magnesium are the main minerals and the others such as zinc and iodine are known as trace elements and are needed only in tiny amounts.

Calcium

This is vital for healthy bones, teeth and nerves, and vitamin D must be present for its proper absorption. Lack of calcium can result in nervous exhaustion, insomnia and cramps. Pregnant and breastfeeding women and those on the contraceptive pill, cortisone and steroid drugs have a particular need.

Some sources of Calcium
Almonds • Brazil nuts • Brie • Camembert • Cheddar and similar cheeses Dried figs • Eggs • Milk • Parmesan • Parsley • Sesame seeds Soy flour • Spinach • Watercress • Yogurt

Iron

This mineral carries oxygen around the body and also plays a part in the formation of red blood cells. Its absorption is enhanced by vitamin C eaten at the same meal. Lack of iron leads to anemia, fatigue, poor memory.

Some sources of Iron
Almonds • Baked (haricot) beans • Bran • Brazil nuts • Cashew nuts Chickpeas/garbanzos • Cocoa • Curry powder • Dried apricots, figs, peaches, prunes, raisins • Eggs • Hazelnuts • Lentils • Millet Molasses • Oatmeal and whole grains • Parsley • Pumpkin, sesame and sunflower seeds • Soy beans • Soy flour • Spinach • Yeast extract

Sodium and potassium

These are the minerals which control the body's water balance. Sodium (salt) is commonly eaten to excess in Western diets and this condition is linked to kidney disorders and high blood pressure with its risks of strokes and heart attacks. Too much sodium inhibits the absorption of potassium. Lack of potassium can lead to heart attacks. Potassium is found in many foods but can easily be destroyed when vegetables are overcooked. Deficiency can occur when little raw food is eaten and the diet is high in refined foods and salt.

Some sources of Potassium
Almonds • Bran • Brazil nuts • Dried apricots • Dried figs Dried peaches • Molasses • Parsley • Prunes • Raisins Soy flour • Sultanas • Yeast extract

Magnesium

Needed to retain potassium in the cells, magnesium also aids the functioning of vitamin B6. Lack of it leads to muscle cramps, nervous depression and convulsions, but deficiency is rare.

Some sources of Magnesium
Almonds • Bran • Brazil nuts • Chickpeas/garbanzos • Dried apricots Haricot beans • Millet • Oatmeal • Peanuts • Soy flour • Walnuts Spinach • Wheatgerm • Wholewheat flour/bread

Phosphorus

Essential for bones and teeth, this mineral is involved in the use of B vitamins. It is found in many foods, especially those which are good sources of calcium.

Zinc

Present in many foods but not always readily absorbed. Although its exact role is not completely defined, deficiency can result in stunted growth, infertility and slow healing of wounds. Low zinc levels are found in people with high blood pressure, women who are pregnant or on contraceptive pills, and heavy drinkers.

Some sources of Zinc
Almonds • Bran • Brazil nuts • Brie and similar cheeses Cheddar and similar cheeses • Hazelnuts • Oatmeal • Parmesan Rye flour • Walnuts • Wholewheat flour/bread

Iodine

Non-vegetarians can obtain iodine from fish. It is also found in dairy products, and in vegetables but here the amount will depend on how much iodine was present in the soil where the vegetables grew. Iodine is an essential part of some hormones and deficiency can lead to thyroid gland disease, a high blood cholesterol level and impaired mental and physical functioning.

Some sources of Iodine
Cheese • Eggs • Milk • Nuts • Olive oil • Onions • Seaweed Watercress • Wholemeal bread • Yogurt

There are many other minerals needed in only tiny amounts and these will be ingested when you eat other foods. In general you do not need to worry about the quantity of vitamins and minerals unless you are on a strict diet for medical reasons.

Sources: The Sixth World Food Survey, Food and Agriculture Organization, Rome 1996; The UK Vegetarian Society; The Vegetarian Resource Group.

Tips for vegetarian meals

- Choose a variety of foods, including whole grains, vegetables, fruits, legumes, nuts, seeds, and dairy products and eggs (for non vegans).
- Choose whole, unrefined foods often and minimize intake of sweetened, fatty and refined foods.
- Choose a variety of fruits and vegetables.
- If eating dairy products, select low-fat versions. Cheeses and other high-fat dairy foods and eggs should be limited in the diet because of their saturated fat content and because their frequent use displaces plant foods in some vegetarian diets.
- Vegans should include a regular source of vitamin B^{12} in their diets, and also a source of vitamin D if sun exposure is limited.
- Solely breast-fed babies should have iron supplements after 4-6 months and, if exposure to sun is limited, a source of vitamin D. Breast-fed vegan infants should have vitamin B^{12} supplements if the mother's diet is not fortified.
- Do not restrict dietary fat in children under 2 years old. For older children include some foods higher in unsaturated fats (such as nuts, seeds, nut/seed butters, avocado and vegetable oils) to help meet nutrient and energy needs.

Vegetarian meal planning

Fats, oils and sweeteners - use these sparingly
Cookies, sweets, butter, margarine, salad dressing, cooking oil

Yogurt, milk and cheese group - 0-3 servings daily*
yogurt - 1 cup (= 1 serving) • milk - 1 cup (eg in tea, coffee or on cereal) • cheese - 1½ oz/35 g
*Vegans need to select from other food sources rich in calcium eg chickpeas, black beans, baked beans, soy foods, almonds, dried figs, greens.

Dried beans, lentils, nuts, seeds, eggs and protein group - 2-3 servings daily
soy milk - 1 cup (= 1 serving) • cooked beans or peas - ½ cup • 1 egg or 2 egg whites • nuts or seeds - 2 tablespoons
tofu or tempeh - ½ cup • peanut butter - 2 tablespoons

Vegetable group - 3-5 servings daily
cooked or chopped raw vegetables - ½ cup (= 1 serving) • raw leafy vegetables - 1 cup

Fruit group - 2-4 servings daily
juice - ½ cup (= 1 serving) • dried fruit - ½ cup • chopped raw fruit - ½ cup • 1 banana, apple or orange

Bread, cereal, rice and pasta group - 6-11 servings daily
bread - 1 slice (= 1 serving) • breakfast cereal - 1 oz/25 g • cooked cereal - ½ cup
cooked rice, pasta or other grains - ½ cup • bagel - ½

American Dietetic Association 1997

Recipe Notes

Roadside stall, Dominican Republic.

PHOTO: N. DURRELL-MCKENNA / HUTCHISON

Recipe Notes

Useful tips and explanations - it is helpful to read these before starting to cook. Before preparing a recipe, read it through to the end. It is usually a good idea to assemble all the ingredients you are going to need before you embark on preparation.

Measures

All measures in the book are given in US cups and metric amounts. While teaspoon measures are the same, British tablespoon measures are larger than in North America and Australasia. British users should therefore use only a scant tablespoon amount. Where American and British spellings differ, we use the American version in this book.

Measures for sugar in this book are given as guide amounts only: if you want to use less or none, that is up to you. If you prefer to cut out the salt, then go ahead. With cooking oil, a specific measure is not usually given. The aim is to use as little as you can (given that most of us in the West eat too much fat - see **Nutrition Guide**, p 21). That amount can vary according to the type of pan you are using: a heavy pan will not require as much cooking oil as a light one. One to two tablespoons are sufficient for most dishes.

Deciding for yourself how much fat or salt to use is important not just for your health but also because the idea of being flexible about what you put into a pot is a useful, some say essential, part of cooking - to test, to add or take out something. This approach also reflects the way most people cook in the developing world where recipe books are few and far between and some of the best cooking goes on at home with hand-me-down favorites. So while each recipe gives the measures for the main ingredients, feel free to experiment.

Names for some ingredients may be different in your country, but we have tried to give a second common name where appropriate. See also the **Ingredients Gallery** (p17) and **Glossary** (p167).

Beans, peas and lentils (pulses or legumes)

The measures given in the recipes are for canned, frozen or cooked ones, **except** for lentils which are given as dry measures. If you want to use dried beans, remember that as a guideline, dried beans will roughly double in weight after soaking so you will need to adjust the quantity and cooking methods. Dried beans should be soaked for 8-12 hours before cooking, and then they should be boiled rapidly for the first 10 minutes to destroy any toxins before you continue to cook them as normal. Soy beans need to boil hard for the first hour. A basic pressure cooker is very useful for cooking beans quickly.

Cooking times for selected pulses

The pulses below need soaking for 8-12 hours (overnight) before cooking, except those marked *. See also packet instructions.

Bean/pulse	Approximate cooking time	In pressure cooker
Aduki beans	45 minutes	15 minutes
Black beans	1 hour	20 minutes
Black-eyed beans/cowpeas	50 minutes	15 minutes
Borlotti beans	1½ hours	25 minutes
Broad beans	1½ hours	40 minutes
Butter or Lima beans	1½ hours	20 minutes
Cannellini beans	50 minutes	15 minutes
Chickpeas/garbanzos	1½ hours	30 minutes
Flageolet beans	50 minutes	20 minutes
Haricot beans	50 minutes	20 minutes
Mung beans	45 minutes	15 minutes
Mung dal *	30 minutes	—
Pigeon peas (Gunga)	45 minutes	15 minutes
Pinto beans	50 minutes	20 minutes
Red kidney beans	1 hour	20 minutes
Rosecoco beans	50 minutes	20 minutes
Soy beans	2½ hours	50 minutes
Whole green peas	1½ hours	30 minutes
Split peas *	45 minutes	—
Whole lentils *	45 minutes	15 minutes
Split lentils *	20 minutes	—
Toor dal *	30 minutes	—
Urad dal *	30 minutes	—

Bulgur and cracked wheat
If using bulgur, pour boiling water over it and leave to soak for about 10 minutes, then drain and use. For cracked wheat, boil for 20 minutes and then let it stand in the pan for a few minutes more, or cook these items according to the instructions on the packet.

Chilis, chili powder, curry powder, other spices and herbs
The measures given for these ingredients are **guide amounts** only, and in the recipes the seeds can be removed to lessen the potency. If you are not sure how hot you like something, or if the spice or herb is unfamiliar, start by using a little and add more later if you wish. In general, food tastes better if you use fresh spices and herbs.

If the chili is not broken or chopped, and therefore the seeds do not get into the dish, then the chili will not make it hot but will impart a smoky flavor. Discard the chili before serving if desired. In the recipes, unless specified otherwise, use the slender red or green chilis which are about 3 inches/7.5 cm long. *Always take care when handling chilis as the hot ingredient, capsaicin, is an irritant. Wash your hands carefully and avoid touching your face.*

Coconut milk
An essential ingredient in many dishes around the world, coconut milk gives a fragrance and richness to foods. It is available in canned, powdered or creamed form. You can also prepare it using desiccated/shredded coconut mixed with water, although this may not be as rich or give the same well-rounded flavor as the other types.

Couscous
Cook according to packet instructions.

Fat and oil
In general, the recipes do not specify the amount of oil or fat to use. The advice is to use as little as possible to begin with and add further small amounts if necessary. Most recipes call simply for 'margarine' or 'oil'. Here it is best to use varieties high in polyunsaturated fat such as corn, safflower, sunflower or soy bean (but soy oil may be made from genetically-modified soybeans; see **Introduction**, p12). Peanut and other high-temperature oils are best for quick frying. If you want to use red palm oil or dendê, coconut oil or ghee (clarified butter), remember that these are high in saturated fats and should not be eaten frequently or in large amounts. However for special occasions you may like to use these ingredients for their characteristic flavor. Vegetable ghee is sometimes available.

You can use a wok or frying pan for most of the frying required in these recipes. Drain fried food on absorbent paper towels where possible. Remember that there is fat in cheese and snack foods such as chips and crackers. Many processed foods are made with saturated fats.

Fiber
Fruit, vegetables, pulses or legumes (beans, peas and so on), seeds and whole grains provide different kinds of fiber. Oats, for example, provide soluble fiber which may help reduce cholesterol levels. Where possible, eat brown rice or pasta and wholemeal/wholewheat flour as well as fresh fruit, seeds, legumes and raw or lightly-cooked vegetables.

Flour
Unless specified otherwise, 'flour' in the recipes means wheat flour. You can use wholemeal/wholewheat interchangeably with refined, or use half and half but bear in mind that wholemeal/wholewheat flour makes a more solid product. It is a good idea to sieve it as this helps aerate it. Just tip the remaining bran in afterwards. Mixing in some soy flour is a good way to increase the protein content of a dish especially for children: one part soy to three parts of wheat flour is fine for most general uses. Soy and rice flour are also good substitutes for people who cannot tolerate the gluten in wheat (but see note on **Genetically Modified Organisms** below). If you find wholemeal/wholewheat pastry difficult to roll out for a pie base, then put the mixture into the pie-dish and press it into place with a metal spoon.

Fruit and vegetables
With concern about fiber on the one hand and anxiety about pesticide residues on the other, it is difficult to advise how to prepare the fruit and vegetables you will be using. Organically-grown produce is obviously the best, if you can obtain it. *In the recipes, it is assumed these items are washed and peeled as desired.*

Genetically Modified Organisms (GMOs)
Many foods now on sale contain GMOs. In some countries such foods have to be clearly labelled but in other places this

is inadequate, or non-existent. Some of the foods widely favored by vegetarians, such as soy beans and other soy products are among the crops where genetic manipulation is widespread (see also **Introduction**, p 12). Vegetarian (and most other) cheeses contain a GM enzyme, chymosin, approved by the Vegetarian Society. It replaces rennet, the enzyme from calves stomachs. Chymosin may be listed as 'enzymes' on the label.

Grains

Unrefined cereals (whole grains) contain the germ, which is the source of oils, proteins and minerals. The bran is an important source of fiber. Grains can be bought in many forms such as whole or cracked, toasted or parboiled.

Cooking times for selected grains

The chart gives an idea of preparation and cooking times, but refer also to the packet instructions.

Grain	Liquid per cup of grain	Approximate cooking time	In pressure cooker
Barley	4 cups	1 hour	20 minutes
Buckwheat	3 cups	20 minutes	8 minutes
Corn/maize	4 cups	5-10 minutes	—
Millet	3 cups	20 minutes	8 minutes
Oats	3 cups	30 minutes	12 minutes
Quinoa	2 cups	15 minutes	—
Rice (brown)	2 cups	30 minutes	10 minutes
Wild rice	3 cups	1 hour	20 minutes

Nuts and seeds

Amounts given for these are for **shelled but raw** (unroasted) items, unless stated otherwise. See also **Toasting/roasting** below. Some people are allergic to nuts.

Peppers/bell peppers

Where a recipe lists bell peppers these are the large sweet red or green varieties.

Plantains/green (savory) bananas

These are easier to peel if you boil them first for about 20 minutes. If you have to peel them before cooking, cut the plantain in half and then make lengthwise cuts in each section and remove the peel.

Rice

Where rice is listed as a main ingredient, Basmati rice has been used because it is both quick to cook and also imparts a delicious fragrance. However, if you have time most recipes can be made with brown rice which, being unpolished, retains its full complement of nutrients.

Salt

Most of us consume too much salt, often in processed foods. The recipes do not specify how much salt to put in: this is up to you. Some people prefer not to use salt at all when cooking, but to let people add their own when the meal is served.

Stock or water

Use stock if possible as it gives a much better flavor to the dish. Vegetarian stock cubes are available, or make your own stock using either Vegemite/Marmite and/or vegetables.

Sugar and Honey

Where sugar is listed as an ingredient, the measure is given as a **guide amount**. You may prefer to reduce or even omit it altogether. Remember, brown sugar is no more virtuous than white. Honey can be substituted where appropriate. It contains somewhat fewer calories than sugar but its tooth-rotting qualities are much the same.

Tamarind

This useful flavoring is now available as a paste or in powdered form. Follow the packet instructions to make up the required amount.

Toasting/roasting

To toast grains, nuts and seeds, broil or grill them, gently shaking them often. You can also put them in a heavy shallow pan, without oil, and heat them on a low fire until they go a shade darker (or follow individual recipe instructions).

Starters, Snacks & Soups

Corn on the cob seller, Bangalore, India.

PHOTO: DARIUSZ KLEMENS

Avocado salad with ginger

Vegan

Serves 2

PREPARATION 5 MINUTES

0 COOKING

Some of Côte d'Ivoire's best and cheapest food is served in the small restaurants or *maquis* (from the French word for scrub or bush, and the name of the French underground resistance in World War Two). The name maquis was originally given to hidden (illegal) drinking haunts in Côte d'Ivoire.

This salad has an exciting taste - smooth-tasting avocado meets sparky ginger. The ground ginger distributes very evenly in the lime or lemon juice, but fresh ginger is tangier.

INGREDIENTS

- 1 avocado, halved and stoned
- 1 tablespoon lime or lemon juice
- 1/2 teaspoon ground ginger or 1/4 teaspoon fresh ginger, finely chopped
- salt

1 Remove the skin from the avocado and cut the fruit into cubes.

2 Mix the lime or lemon juice in a bowl with the ginger, and a little salt. Place the avocado cubes into the dressing and mix carefully before serving with hot bread ◆

Lentil salad

Vegan

Serves 2-3

PREPARATION
10
MINUTES
15
COOKING

Because Ethiopia mainly hits the headlines only with its food shortages and border wars, it is sometimes hard to remember that this country has one of the richest culinary traditions. Most people are Coptic Christians and follow a non-meat diet on fasting days - and anyway meat is expensive (beef is exported to Europe). So the *wats* (stews) made of lentils, and spiced with *berberé* paste are popular. This is a salad version.

INGREDIENTS

1 cup / 150 g red lentils
1 tablespoon grated onion
1/2 teaspoon chili powder
juice of 1 lemon
oil
salt and pepper

1. Put the lentils into a bowl and cover with boiling water. Set aside for 10 minutes. Drain.
2. Transfer the lentils to a pan and pour over boiling water to cover them well. Cover, bring to the boil and simmer for 15 minutes until soft.
3. While the lentils are cooking, mix the onion with the lemon juice, chili powder, oil, salt and pepper in a bowl.
4. When the lentils are ready, drain; rinse in cold water to cool and then drain again thoroughly. Place them in the bowl with the dressing, and combine well ◆

Avocado dip

Long before the US civil war, white US slaveholders had a 'problem' with emancipated blacks. One 'solution' was to 'repatriate' them to Africa. In 1821 part of British Sierra Leone was purchased to form Liberia (liberation) and its capital named Monrovia after the US President James Monroe. The 20,000 or so black settlers were heavily supported by the US, and became a local elite with better land and more clout than the African people already living there.

Vegan

Serves 4

INGREDIENTS

2 avocados, stoned and halved
juice of half a lime or lemon
dash of Tabasco or chili sauce
salt and pepper

1 Scoop the avocado into a bowl and mash it with a fork.

2 Now pour in the lime juice and Tabasco sauce and stir well.

3 Season, and serve with hot toast, bread or sliced bell peppers ◆

Banana soup

Serves 4-6

PREPARATION
5
MINUTES
15
COOKING

Malawi's name means 'the lake where the sun's haze is reflected in the water like fire'. The country has tall mountains, wide plains, forests and of course the huge lake - in the Rift fault - which stretches along its borders with Tanzania and Mozambique. In this recipe, you can use yellow (ripe) bananas which make this an intriguing mixture between a savory and a dessert.

INGREDIENTS

4 bananas, peeled
3 cups / 700 ml milk (keep 2 tablespoons back)
grated peel and juice of 1/2 orange
1/4 teaspoon cinnamon
1 teaspoon sugar
1 tablespoon cornstarch/cornflour
salt

1. For best results put the peeled bananas and milk into a liquidizer. Alternatively, mash bananas well. Then gradually pour in the milk, beating to make a smooth mixture.
2. Transfer the mix to a pan and add sugar and salt to taste, and put in the orange peel and juice.
3. Cover and bring to the boil; then reduce the heat and simmer for 5 minutes.
4. Blend the cornstarch/cornflour with the retained milk to make a smooth paste and pour this into the soup, stirring well. Cook for 2 minutes until the soup thickens slightly and then serve hot or cold, with the cinnamon sprinkled over ◆

Papaya/pawpaw soup

Down to the east of the highveld is South Africa's warm, sub-tropical region where much of the citrus fruit is grown. Along the coastline of KwaZulu-Natal and the Eastern Cape are the sugar and banana plantations - and papaya/pawpaw trees.

Serves 4-6

INGREDIENTS

- 1 pound / 450 g papaya/pawpaw *
- 1 cup / 240 ml papaya/pawpaw juice * or orange juice
- 1 onion, finely chopped
- 2 cups / 480 ml milk
- 1 teaspoon cornstarch/cornflour
- 1/2 teaspoon nutmeg
- 1 tablespoon fresh cilantro/coriander or parsley, chopped
- oil
- salt and pepper

* If using canned papaya/pawpaw in syrup, drain and rinse the fruit well. If in juice, retain the juice.

1. To begin, heat the oil and fry the onion for 5-10 minutes until it is cooked.
2. While the onion is frying, prepare the papaya (if using fresh). Cut it in half and remove the seeds. Peel and then chop the fruit finely.
3. Add the pawpaw and juice to the onions. Shake in the nutmeg, salt and pepper, and cook for 5-8 minutes. Then mash the papaya with a fork.
4. Thicken the soup as desired by mixing the cornstarch/cornflour with a little water and then adding this paste to the soup. Add the cilantro/coriander, stir well and cook for 2-3 minutes.
5. Pour in the milk and heat through, taking care that it does not boil, for a few minutes before serving ◆

Peanut soup

Serves 2-4

PREPARATION
10
MINUTES
10
COOKING

Uganda's former dictator, Idi Amin, today lives in relative splendor in Saudi Arabia as a guest of the royal household. Instead of his army uniform and medals, he now dons Arab dress and tends his goats, chickens and vegetables.

Peanuts, or groundnuts as they are often known, are common food in Uganda. They are legumes which grow underground, and are rich in protein. This dish is full of distinctively African flavors.

INGREDIENTS

- 1 cup / 225 g peanuts
- 1/4 onion
- 2 cups / 480 ml vegetable stock
- 1 cup / 240 ml milk
- 1 tablespoon cornstarch/cornflour
- 1/2 teaspoon chili powder or 1/2 red chili, de-seeded and finely chopped
- salt

1. Start by blending the peanuts and the onion in a blender.
2. Then mix the cornstarch/cornflour with a little of the milk. Transfer this to a large pan, and slowly pour in the remaining milk while stirring constantly to make a smooth mixture.
3. Now add the stock, ground peanuts and onion, chili and salt, stirring as you do so. Cover the pan and bring to the boil; then simmer for 5 minutes.
4. Mix well, or blend, to ensure the ingredients are well combined and then serve ◆

Pumpkin soup

Many South Pacific recipes, and a lot of South Indian ones, use coconut milk - which makes it a popular ingredient in many of the dishes served in our part-South Indian/part-European/Fiji Islands family. Coconut milk is now easily obtainable in ordinary shops in many places. This is a basic "European"-style recipe for pumpkin soup, but don't go mad with too much ginger as it can overpower the delicate pumpkin and coconut flavors.

Seona Smiles, Suva, Fiji Islands

Vegan adaptable

Serves 4

INGREDIENTS

- 1 pound / 450 g pumpkin, peeled and finely chopped
- 1 onion, finely sliced
- ½ teaspoon fresh ginger, finely chopped
- 2 tablespoons butter or margarine
- 2½ cups / 600 ml stock or water
- 2 cups / 480 ml coconut milk
- 1 tablespoon fresh parsley or cilantro/coriander, chopped
- salt and pepper

1. Put the butter or margarine in a saucepan and heat until it melts. Stir-fry the onion and ginger for a few minutes, then add the pumpkin and stir-fry for a further 2-3 minutes.
2. Now pour in the stock or water. Bring to the boil, then let simmer for 15-20 minutes, until the pumpkin is soft. Blend or mash the pumpkin to make a purée.
3. Add the coconut milk and gently reheat the soup, taking care that it does not boil. Season, and garnish with the herbs before serving ◆

Mushrooms with cardamom

Vegan

Serves 2

PREPARATION
10
MINUTES

3
COOKING

Cardamoms grow in the eponymous hills of southern India. The pods containing the seeds lie at the base of the tall plant, with tiny pink and white flowers signalling their whereabouts. Cardamom's exotic flavor blends well with the lemon in this light dish, and the turmeric gives it a golden hue.

INGREDIENTS

1/2 pound / 225 g mushrooms, finely chopped
1 clove garlic, crushed
seeds of 2 cardamoms, crushed
1/2 inch/1 cm fresh ginger, finely chopped or 1/2 teaspoon ground ginger
1/4 teaspoon turmeric
juice of 1/2 lime or lemon
oil
salt and pepper

1. Start by mixing together the garlic, cardamom seeds, ginger, turmeric, lime or lemon juice and seasoning.
2. Place the mushrooms in a bowl and pour the mixture over, turning the mushrooms well to coat them.
3. Now heat the oil in a wok or pan and stir-fry the mushrooms for 1-3 minutes until they are cooked ◆

Brinjal purée

EGG-PLANT/AUBERGINE AND COCONUT MILK PURÉE

Brinjal, egg-plant, garden egg, aubergine - these are just some of the names by which this popular purple vegetable is known around the world. It turns up in many recipes, and its versatility is welcomed in vegetarian dishes. This purée is good with pittas or raw vegetables cut into sticks.

Vegan

Serves 2

PREPARATION **5** MINUTES **15** COOKING

INGREDIENTS

- 1 egg-plant/aubergine, halved
- 1 cup / 240 ml coconut milk
- 1 clove garlic, crushed
- 1/2 teaspoon ground ginger or fresh, finely chopped
- 1/4 teaspoon chili powder
- salt

1. Make slits in the egg-plant/aubergine skin and cook under the grill for 10-15 minutes or so, turning often so that it softens all over.
2. When it is done, chop finely, or put in the blender, with all the other ingredients, adding more coconut milk if necessary. Serve with toast or hot breads ◆

Mrs Hasimoto's miso soup

Vegan

Serves 4-6

PREPARATION
10
MINUTES
10
COOKING

Miso - fermented soy paste - is a staple food in Japan, and is eaten as soup with almost every meal at any time of the day or night. It can range from a light dish to a more substantial stew-type creation. The most simple soup usually has some type of green cabbage (eg *bak choi* or Chinese cabbage) diced beancurd/tofu and some chopped scallions/spring onions. Vegetables that can be used are potatoes, carrots, onions, pumpkin, green cabbage, Chinese lettuce, beansprouts and spinach. Traditionally this soup contains *dashi* which is a light fish stock but for the vegetarian version, dried seaweed (such as *wakame* or *nori*) can be substituted. Miso is considered great for the digestion and is extremely nutritious.

Sarah Byham, Tokyo, Japan

INGREDIENTS

3 cups / 750 ml water *

¼ cup / 60 g miso *

¼ pound / 110 g beancurd/tofu, diced

1 cup / 150 g mixed vegetables, finely chopped

1 teaspoon dried seaweed

* Use ⅔ cup/150 ml water + 15g of fresh miso per single serving, but for larger quantities you need proportionately less miso, eg for 7-8 servings you would need 1 litre water + 85g of miso. Experiment to find the proportion that suits you.

1. First, bring the water to the boil. Now add the beancurd /tofu and the vegetables, excluding those that cook quickly like spinach, cabbage and beansprouts. Cook until they become soft.
2. When the vegetables are ready, add the quick-cooking ones and the seaweed, for a few minutes and then turn off the heat.
3. Stir in the miso, mixing thoroughly, and then serve ◆

Kai tom kah

MUSHROOM SOUP WITH LEMON GRASS

The usual version contains chicken, but the flavors of this delicious soup combine happily with mushrooms or bamboo shoots. Despite the long list of ingredients, this is fairly quick to make, and certainly worth the time. Laos powder, also known as galangal, comes from a rhizome found in Southeast Asia, and can be bought in Chinese or other specialty stores, as can lemon grass.

Vegan

Serves 4

PREPARATION **10** MINUTES

20 COOKING

INGREDIENTS

½ pound / 225 g mushrooms, thinly sliced

2 cups / 480 ml coconut milk

3 stalks lemon grass, cut into 2-inch/5-cm lengths or 1 tablespoon dried lemon grass, soaked

4 teaspoons laos powder/galangal or 4 thin slices fresh galangal

1 chili, de-seeded and finely chopped

4 lime or lemon leaves or grated rind of 1 lime or lemon

1 cup / 240 ml water

2 tablespoons fresh cilantro/coriander, chopped

juice of 1 lime or lemon

salt

1. Pour the coconut milk into a pan or wok and add the mushrooms, lemon grass, laos powder and chili. Bring gently to the boil and then simmer over a gentle heat for 5 minutes.
2. When ready, add the water, lime or lemon leaves (or rind) and 1 tablespoon of the cilantro/coriander leaves. Season, and stir to combine the ingredients as they cook together gently for 10 minutes.
3. Before serving, scatter the remaining cilantro/coriander leaves on top, and hand round the lime or lemon juice separately ◆

Sweetcorn soup

Serves 2

PREPARATION
5
MINUTES
20
COOKING

Antigua was first inhabited by Carib indians, but most left - like the Spanish and French who followed them - because of the lack of water. A few English eventually settled in the 17th century, having cracked the water storage problem - and killed any remaining indians. African slaves were then imported to work the tobacco and sugar plantations.

INGREDIENTS

- 2 cups / 450 g sweetcorn
- 1 onion, finely chopped
- 2 cups / 480 ml milk
- 1 tablespoon flour
- 1/2 teaspoon nutmeg
- oil
- salt and pepper

1. Using a saucepan, sauté the onion in the oil for about 10 minutes, and when it is golden add the flour. Mix well and cook for 1 minute. Season.
2. Now pour in half the milk, a little at a time, and stir constantly to make a thick mixture. Cook for 1 minute.
3. Next, add the sweetcorn and nutmeg, and stir as the soup simmers for 5 minutes. Transfer to the blender and blend, pouring in the remaining milk to make the desired consistency. Heat through without boiling ◆

Carrot, tomato and orange soup

Seven countries make up Central America, and their foods reflect their histories. Guatemala, Belize and Honduras were part of the old Mayan empire, as was El Salvador. The Aztec empire also left its mark, but not as deeply as the Spanish conquest. Food in these countries is similar to that of Mexico - corn/maize, tomatoes, chilis - while in Nicaragua, Costa Rica and Panama the cuisine shows the influence of Colombia with bananas, coconuts and root vegetables. This soup has a bright color and a tangy, fresh taste.

Vegan

Serves 4

PREPARATION **5** MINUTES

25 COOKING

INGREDIENTS

6 tomatoes, chopped
1 carrot, finely sliced
1 onion, finely sliced
1 teaspoon dry basil
½ teaspoon sugar
2½ cups / 600 ml stock
1 cup / 240 ml orange juice
oil
salt and pepper

1. Heat oil in a large pan and sauté the onion for 5-8 minutes until it is golden.
2. Now add the tomatoes, carrot, basil and sugar, and cook together for 5 minutes, stirring well.
3. When ready, pour in the stock and then bring the pan to the boil, reduce the heat, and simmer for 10 minutes.
4. Put the mixture into the blender; return it to the pan and add orange juice to taste; season. Heat through before serving ◆

Avocado and egg snack

Vegan adaptable
Serves 2

PREPARATION 5 MINUTES
10 COOKING

This has an interesting flavor, with the sour vinegar and the tang of chili combining well. The egg makes this a substantial snack, but it could be omitted for a lighter bite or for a vegan meal.

INGREDIENTS

- 1 avocado, halved and stoned
- 1 egg
- 1 scallion/spring onion, chopped
- 1 tablespoon fresh parsley, chopped
- 1/4-1/2 teaspoon fresh red chili, de-seeded or 1/4 teaspoon chili powder
- 2-4 teaspoons vinegar
- salt

1. First, put on the egg to boil for 8-10 minutes and then cool under cold water. Peel and chop.
2. While it is boiling, scoop out the avocado into a bowl and mash it with a fork.
3. Add the chopped egg, onion, parsley, chili, vinegar and salt and mix well. Then either pile back into the avocado shells, or serve on toast ◆

Aguacates rellenos

STUFFED AVOCADOS

The early Mexicans were busy cultivating peppers, squash and avocados some 9,000 years ago - about the same time as their counterparts in the Middle East. Two thousand years later they were growing maize/sweetcorn and beans, and around 700 AD came tomato cultivation. These crops still play a central part in Mexican food.

This dish is quick to make and very refreshing. In summer time, when lighter meals go down well, it could make a main dish.

Vegan

Serves 4

PREPARATION **5** MINUTES

0 COOKING

INGREDIENTS

2 avocados, halved and stoned
1 tablespoon sweetcorn
1/2 green bell pepper, finely chopped
2 tomatoes, finely chopped
1/2 teaspoon chili powder
1 clove garlic, crushed
juice of 1/2 lemon
oil
salt and pepper

1 Combine the corn with the bell pepper and tomatoes in a bowl.

2 Mix the dressing of oil, lemon juice, garlic, salt and pepper and then pour this over the salad vegetables, stirring well.

3 Heap the mixture onto the avocados and sprinkle lightly with chili powder before serving ◆

Nachos

Serves 2-4

PREPARATION
5
MINUTES
10
COOKING

Nachos dishes are now widespread as a popular snack. Luckily for many of us, we do not have to grind the maize flour and make the corn chips... Still, we can grate the cheese and prepare a lip-smacking snack. If you like, mash up an avocado pear with some lemon juice and serve that also.

INGREDIENTS

- 1 pack tortilla chips
- 1 pound / 450 g Monterey Jack or cheddar cheese, grated
- 2-4 pickled jalepeño chilis, de-seeded and finely sliced or gherkins, sliced lengthwise
- 1/2 cup / 110 ml yogurt or sour cream
- 1/4 teaspoon chili powder or 1/2 teaspoon paprika
- lemon or lime wedges

Heat oven to 400°F/200°C/Gas 6

1. Scatter the tortilla chips on a baking sheet and grate the cheese over to cover well.
2. Arrange the jalepeños or gherkins on top and then place in the oven. Bake for 5 minutes or until the cheese is melted.
3. Sprinkle the chili powder or paprika on top and then serve with lemon or lime wedges and yogurt or sour cream ◆

Lentil soup

Indians from the subcontinent were brought in as indentured labor for the sugar plantations in the 19th century, after the ending of slavery meant that Africans could move to the cities. Indian influence is marked in Trinidad, especially in the use of masala pastes and ghee (clarified butter). Caribbean people island-hop, and their cuisines draw frequently from one another.

Serves 2-4

PREPARATION **5** MINUTES **30** COOKING

INGREDIENTS

- 1 cup / 150 g red lentils
- 1 onion, finely chopped
- 1/2 teaspoon chili powder
- 1 cup / 240 ml milk
- oil
- salt

1. Soak the lentils in boiling water for 10 minutes. Drain. Then put them in a pan, cover with boiling water and cook for 15 minutes or until soft.
2. While that is happening, heat the oil and cook the onion gently, adding the chili powder after 5 minutes. Stir and cook for a further 3-5 minutes. Add the cooked lentils with their cooking liquid and stir to mix well.
3. Spoon the onion mixture and lentils, together with the milk and salt into the blender and whizz until everything is combined and the desired consistency. Return the soup to the pan and heat through before serving ◆

Gibneh beyda

CHEESE PATÉ

Serves 2-4

PREPARATION
5
MINUTES

0
COOKING

This cheese paté from Egypt is delicious on pitta bread. Feta cheese, made from goat's or sheep's milk is a popular cheese in Mediterranean countries such as Greece, Italy - and Egypt. It tends to be quite salty as it is cured and stored in salt water and whey. You can reduce the salt by rinsing the cheese or soaking it in milk for about an hour. Olive oil is best for this dish, and so is thick yogurt.

Pippa Pearce, London

INGREDIENTS

- ½ pound / 225 g feta cheese
- 1½ cups / 330 ml yogurt
- 2 tablespoons fresh mint, finely chopped
- 2 tablespoons fresh parsley, finely chopped
- 2 tablespoons fresh dill, finely chopped
- juice of ½ lemon
- 1 tablespoon oil
- pepper

1. In a bowl, mash the feta with a fork, and then beat in the yogurt to make a smooth mixture (or use a blender).
2. Now scatter in the mint, parsley and dill and pour in the lemon juice. Combine well. Taste the mixture: usually the feta is salty enough to carry the dish but add salt if desired.
3. Pour the oil over, and grind fresh black pepper on top. Serve with hot pitta bread and olives ◆

Hummus

GARBANZO/CHICKPEA DIP

Vegan adaptable

Serves 4

PREPARATION **10** MINUTES

0 COOKING

'I have heard, in the old days, Baghdadi women and cooks jeer at Syrians [neighbors in Baghdad] for being very economical with meat: all those salads and pastes that were being introduced in Iraq, *tabbouleh, homus, baba-ghanush,* were only means of saving on meat,' writes Sami Zubaida in *Culinary Cultures of the Middle East*. These dishes are now popular around the world, not least with non-meat eaters.

INGREDIENTS

- 2 cups / 300 g garbanzos/chickpeas, drained (keep liquid)
- 2 teaspoons tahina
- 3 cloves garlic, crushed
- juice of 1/2-1 lemon
- a little milk and/or oil
- 2 tablespoons fresh parsley, chopped
- salt and pepper

1. Place all the ingredients except the milk/oil, parsley and seasoning into a blender.
2. Add 2 tablespoons of retained liquid and whizz until smooth. Pour in milk, oil or more retained liquid as required to make a dipping consistency. Season.
3. Turn the mixture into a serving bowl and scatter the parsley over before serving with pitta bread, chapatis or chopped raw vegetables ◆

Baking traditional bread, Cairo, Egypt.
PHOTO: JEREMY HORNER / HUTCHISON

Garbanzo/chickpea snack

Garbanzos/chickpeas are familiar foods both within and outside their area of origin, the Middle East. But did you know they were also made into soap? A 14th century cookbook by Ibn Razin al-Tujibi tells you how. For this snack meal, it's best to use thick yogurt.

Serves 4

PREPARATION
10
MINUTES

INGREDIENTS

1 cup / 150 g garbanzos/chickpeas, drained
1 tablespoon pine nuts
1-2 cloves garlic, crushed
2 cups / 440 ml yogurt
1 tablespoon fresh mint, chopped
4 pittas
1/4 teaspoon paprika
salt

1 Break the pittas into bite-sized pieces and arrange on a flat dish.

2 Put all the other ingredients into a bowl and mix well. Spoon onto the pitta breads and serve with the paprika sprinkled on top ◆

Hab-el-Jose

WALNUT SNACK

Vegan

Serves 4

PREPARATION
5
MINUTES
5
COOKING

Streets in Middle Eastern countries are full of stalls selling tasty food. Many vendors sell sweet snacks, and ones with nuts like this recipe. In addition to the herbs and spices, it uses tahina paste made from ground sesame seeds to give a special flavor.

Pippa Pearce, London

INGREDIENTS

1 tablespoon sesame seeds
1 cup / 75 g ground walnuts
1/2 cup / 75 g breadcrumbs
1/2 teaspoon ground cumin
1/2 teaspoon chili powder
1/2-1 teaspoon tahina
juice of 1 lemon
2 tablespoons water
1 tablespoon fresh parsley
salt and pepper

1 Put all the ingredients into a blender and mix well, adding more lemon juice and/or water to create the desired taste and consistency. Serve with hot pitta bread ◆

Skordalia me karydia

ALMOND AND GARLIC PASTE

This has a wonderful and intriguing flavor. If you are not a garlic fan, cut down the amount you use as it is very powerful.

Vegan

Serves 4

PREPARATION 5 MINUTES

0 COOKING

INGREDIENTS

1 cup / 125 g ground almonds
3 slices bread
3 tablespoons white wine vinegar
2-4 cloves garlic, crushed
oil
salt

1 First, dampen the bread with a little water.

2 Now mash it with the vinegar and then transfer with all the other ingredients to a blender, using the oil to bring it to the desired consistency. Serve with toast or pitta bread ◆

Muttabal

EGG-PLANT/AUBERGINE DIP

Vegan

Serves 4

PREPARATION 5 MINUTES 15 COOKING

Some of the simplest fast foods are just things you have with bread or dip vegetables into.

Pippa Pearce, London

INGREDIENTS

2 egg-plants/aubergines, halved
2 cloves garlic, crushed
1 teaspoon ground coriander
1 tablespoon tahina
1/2 teaspoon chili powder
1 tablespoon fresh cilantro/coriander, chopped
juice of 1/2 lemon
oil
salt

1. Slash the skin of the egg-plants/aubergines and grill for 10 minutes or until they are soft and collapsing.
2. Let them cool a while, and then chop coarsely and put in the blender with all the other ingredients.
3. Mix well, using a little oil to make a soft consistency ◆

Felafel

GARBANZO/CHICKPEA SNACKS

Felafels are very popular as street-food in the region - the original veggie-burger. This recipe is very simple and makes delicious felafels.

Makes 12

PREPARATION **20** MINUTES

INGREDIENTS

- ½ cup / 110 g bulgur
- 1 cup / 150 g garbanzos/chickpeas
- 3 cloves garlic, crushed
- juice of 1 lemon
- 1 teaspoon ground cumin
- ½ teaspoon chili powder
- 2 eggs
- ½ cup / 50 g dry breadcrumbs
- 3 tablespoons fresh cilantro/coriander, chopped
- oil
- salt

1 To start, place the bulgur in a bowl and pour on enough boiling water to cover. Leave to soak for 20 minutes and then drain, or cook according to packet instructions.

2 Meanwhile put the garbanzos/chickpeas, garlic, lemon juice, cumin, chili powder and salt into a blender and whizz until smooth.

3 In a bowl, beat the eggs and add the breadcrumbs. Mix well before adding the garbanzo/chickpea paste, coriander and drained bulgur. Mix together.

4 Heat a little oil in a frying pan. Shape the felafel mix into patties and when the oil is hot, cook for a few minutes on each side to brown. Drain on kitchen paper, and then serve at once in pitta bread with yogurt and salad ◆

Harira

BEAN SOUP

Vegan

Serves 4-6

PREPARATION **10** MINUTES

30 COOKING

At dusk, crowds stroll around the large Djemma el Fna square in Marrakech, looking at the stalls selling food. Some of what's on sale is definitely not for vegetarians, but you can always find lots of *harira* (bean soup). This is one of Morocco's most popular dishes, particularly during the Muslim fasting month of Ramadan when it is consumed to break the daily fast. It is usually made of garbanzos/chickpeas, lentils and haricot beans but you can substitute others.

INGREDIENTS

- 1 cup / 150 g garbanzos/chickpeas, drained (retain liquid)
- 1 cup / 150 g haricot or other beans, drained (retain liquid)
- 2 cups / 400 g canned tomatoes
- 1 onion, chopped
- 1/2 teaspoon saffron strands, soaked in a little water
- 1/2 teaspoon turmeric
- 1/2 teaspoon cinnamon
- 1 teaspoon ground coriander
- 2 tablespoons fresh cilantro/coriander, chopped
- 2 tablespoons fresh parsley, chopped
- juice of 1/2 lemon
- 1/4-1/2 teaspoon harissa* or chili powder
- 1 tablespoon flour
- oil
- salt and pepper

* Harissa is a fiery paste made from chilis; you can find it in speciality stores.

1. Place the garbanzos/chickpeas, beans, tomatoes and onion into a saucepan, together with the saffron and its water, turmeric, cinnamon, ground coriander, salt and pepper. Add 1 tablespoon each of the fresh cilantro/coriander and parsley, as well as the lemon juice.

2. Now pour in enough water, stock or retained liquid to cover the ingredients in the saucepan. Bring to the boil and then simmer gently for 10-15 minutes until the onion is soft.

3. When ready, remove a little of the liquid and mix it with the flour to make a paste, and then stir this into the soup.

4. Continue to cook the soup for a further 5 minutes or longer if you have time, stirring to blend the ingredients well.

5. Add the harissa or chili powder just before you serve, mixing well. Serve with the remaining parsley and cilantro/coriander scattered on top ◆

Muhamara

HAZELNUT PASTE

Kemal Ataturk, the Turkish reforming leader, tried in the 1920s to get Turks to drink alcohol, both because he thought it was good for them, and also because a wine industry would boost the economy. But he did not succeed: most Turks still prefer to drink coffee and eat grapes, and only a tiny proportion of the country's vast grape harvest is fermented. Olive oil is the best for this dry, tasty nut starter.

Pippa Pearce, London

Serves 2

PREPARATION 5 MINUTES 5 COOKING

INGREDIENTS

1 cup / 75 g hazelnuts, ground
1/4 red chili, de-seeded and crushed
juice of 1/2 lemon
1 tablespoon yogurt
1 tablespoon fresh parsley, chopped
oil
salt

1 First toast the nuts under the grill for 3-4 minutes until they began to turn brown.

2 Then put the nuts, chili, juice, yogurt and salt in the blender, adding enough oil to make a paste. Garnish with parsley and serve on toast or pitta bread ◆

Main Dishes

Ijca Indian cooking plantain, Sierra Nevada de Santa Marta, Colombia.

PHOTO: VICTOR ENGLEBERT / ROBERT HARDING

Vegetables in coconut milk

Restaurants in Congo, capital Brazzaville, provide mostly French cuisine although some do offer African dishes like palm cabbage salad. The French influence in the kitchen is a legacy from colonial times, and some people in the country also detect a legacy of French influence in political matters. Congo's main export is oil, and the agricultural sector has played second fiddle to the petroleum industry.

Vegan

Serves 4-6

PREPARATION **10** MINUTES

15 COOKING

INGREDIENTS

- ½ pound / 225 g cauliflower florets, sliced
- 1 carrot, finely sliced
- 1 potato, finely sliced +
- 1 cup / 120 g peas
- ¼ pound / 110 g green beans
- 1½ cups / 350 ml coconut milk
- ½ teaspoon turmeric
- 1 tablespoon fresh cilantro/coriander, chopped
- salt

+ optional

1. Boil the vegetables in a little water first, starting with the cauliflower, carrot and potato (if using), which take longer to cook. Drain.
2. Heat the coconut milk in the same pan; do not let it boil. Add the turmeric and seasoning, and then the vegetables.
3. Sprinkle in the cilantro/coriander, and then cook gently for 10 minutes to let the flavors develop ◆

Spinach patties

Serves 4

PREPARATION 10 MINUTES

15 COOKING

East Africa as a region encompasses Kenya and Tanzania, but in the early days of independence these two countries decided to link with Uganda to form the East African Economic Community. The plans faltered after the Kenyan government allowed its military installations to be used for the notorious 1976 Israeli raid on Entebbe in Uganda, and the project was dropped in 1977.

INGREDIENTS

- 1/2 pound / 225 g frozen pastry, thawed
- 2 pounds / 900 g fresh spinach, finely chopped *
- 1 onion, grated
- 1/2 pound / 225 g feta, crumbled, or cottage cheese
- 1 teaspoon nutmeg
- 2 eggs, beaten
- salt and pepper

* Frozen or canned spinach may not be suitable as these tend to be very wet; if you use them, drain out most of the moisture after thawing/opening.

Heat oven to 400°F/200°C/Gas 6

1. Roll out the pastry to 1/4 inch/0.5 cm thickness and cut into circles, using a cookie cutter, or a saucer for larger patties.
2. Now mix the spinach (make sure it is dry) with the other ingredients to make a stiff consistency.
3. Spoon some of the mixture on one half of the pastry circle, fold over the other half and press down the edges with a fork. Pierce the patty with a fork. Repeat until all the mix is used up.
4. Place the patties on a baking sheet in the oven and cook for 10-15 minutes until golden brown. Serve with salad ◆

Mushroom and egg-plant/aubergine stew

In the south of Ghana, maize flour is fermented and then made into balls known as *kenkey*, which are steamed and wrapped in maize leaves. These are a popular street food, served with just a dash of ground tomatoes, onions and peppers or fish. According to the *Rough Guide*, Ghana was the first West African country to have a brewery and today it has many beers including Gulder, Star, ABC and Club.

Vegan

Serves 2-4

PREPARATION **10** MINUTES **20** COOKING

INGREDIENTS

- 1 egg-plant/aubergine, diced
- 1/2 pound / 225 g mushrooms, sliced
- 2 tomatoes, chopped
- 1 onion, finely sliced
- 1/4 teaspoon chili, de-seeded and finely chopped, or 1/4 teaspoon chili powder
- 1/2 cup / 120 ml stock from the vegetables (see step1) or water
- oil
- salt

1. First, boil the egg-plant/aubergine pieces in boiling water for 5-10 minutes until soft. Drain, keeping the liquid, and then mash coarsely.
2. While that is happening, sauté the onion in the oil for 5-8 minutes, and then put in the mushrooms, tomatoes, chili and salt. Fry gently until the tomatoes and mushrooms have softened.
3. Now stir in the mashed egg-plant/aubergine and stock, and simmer for 10 minutes. Stir from time to time to produce a thick stew consistency ◆

Corn, bean and spinach mash

Vegan

Serves 4

PREPARATION

5

MINUTES

15

COOKING

Much of Kenya is very dry, and so around three-quarters of the people live on just 10 per cent of the land - mostly in the central highlands area. The high density of population makes heavy demands on land and water resources.

If using canned sweetcorn, drain first; if using frozen, cook according to packet instructions.

INGREDIENTS

2 cups / 300 g sweetcorn

1 cup / 150 g red kidney beans, drained

1 pound / 450 g spinach, chopped

2 potatoes, cubed

1 teaspoon garam masala

1-2 tablespoons fresh cilantro/coriander, chopped

1 tomato, sliced

salt

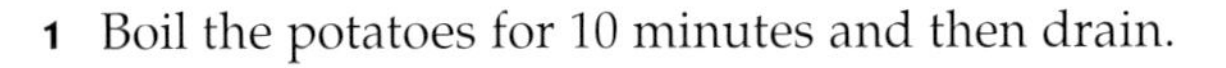

1 Boil the potatoes for 10 minutes and then drain.

2 Using the same pan, heat the sweetcorn and beans gently with the spinach, adding a little water if necessary.

3 When they are hot, add the potatoes, garam masala, cilantro/coriander and salt. Mix well and then cook for 5 minutes, stirring to mash the ingredients. Serve with the slices of tomato on top ◆

KENYA

Garbanzo/chickpea stew

'Old women dark and bent/trudge along with their hoes/to plots of weedy maize' writes Kenyan poet Marina Gashe in *The Village*. Farming is the main occupation for 80 per cent of Kenya's 29 million people; primary and processed agricultural goods contribute over 55 per cent of export earnings. Maize, weedy or not, is the major food crop, followed by sorghum, cassava, beans and fruit.

Vegan

Serves 2-4

PREPARATION **10** MINUTES **30** COOKING

INGREDIENTS

1 cup / 150 g garbanzos/chickpeas
4 tomatoes, chopped
1 onion, chopped
2 cloves garlic, crushed
1 teaspoon ground ginger or ½ teaspoon fresh ginger, finely chopped
1 teaspoon ground cumin
1 teaspoon ground coriander
½ teaspoon chili powder
juice of 1 lemon
2 tablespoons fresh cilantro/coriander, chopped
oil
salt and pepper

1. Heat the oil and sauté the onion for 5-8 minutes. When it is golden, add the garlic, ginger, cumin, ground coriander and chili. Season and stir well.
2. Now put in the tomatoes, and cook for 5-10 minutes, stirring frequently.
3. Next, add the garbanzos/chickpeas together with the lemon juice and cilantro/coriander.
4. Partially mash the mixture with a spoon or potato masher, and heat through for 10-15 minutes before serving ◆

Mushrooms with yogurt

Serves 2-4

PREPARATION

5

MINUTES

20

COOKING

If you ever wondered where those perfect but scent-less single-stem red roses come from, it could be Kenya. Horticultural production gave the economy a boost in 1996, with roses the main bloom. Traditional cash crops like tea and coffee are losing ground after bad droughts and falls in commodity prices.

In this recipe, tomato and yogurt flavors complement each other, and mushrooms go well with the sour taste.

INGREDIENTS

- 1 pound / 450 g mushrooms, finely chopped
- 4 tomatoes, chopped
- 1 onion, finely chopped
- 1 cup / 220 ml yogurt or buttermilk
- oil
- salt

1. First, heat the oil in a heavy pan and sauté the onion before adding the mushrooms. Increase the heat and fry them for 2-3 minutes.
2. Now add the tomatoes and continue to cook for 3 minutes or so, stirring all the time. Remove from the heat and let the mixture stand to cool for 2 minutes.
3. When ready, stir in the yogurt and add salt. Return the pan to the heat and cook gently without boiling (or the yogurt will curdle) for 5 minutes or until the ingredients are well combined ◆

Okra and savory banana (plantain) stew

Okra, also known as ladies' fingers and gumbo, was probably first domesticated in either Ethiopia or West Africa, although it may have originated in Asia. Whatever the plant's origins, it is popular in both African and Indian cuisine. When cooked, okra produces a mucilaginous substance that thickens stews. In this dish, the cooked plantain turns a rich golden orange, so the stew has attractive colors as well as a nice zesty taste.

Vegan

Serves 4-6

PREPARATION **10** MINUTES **30** COOKING

INGREDIENTS

- 20 okras, finely chopped
- 2 savory bananas/ plantains
- 1 cup / 150 g rice
- 8 tomatoes, chopped
- 1 onion, finely chopped
- juice of 1 lime or lemon
- oil
- salt and pepper

1. To begin, place the savory banana unpeeled in a pan of boiling water and boil for 5-8 minutes. At the same time put the rice into another pan and pour boiling water over to cover. Bring to the boil and cook for 10 minutes. Drain.
2. While the plantain and rice are cooking heat the oil and sauté the onion for about 5 minutes.
3. When the plantain is ready, run cold water over it to cool, and then slice the peel lengthwise to remove. Chop the banana/plantain very finely.
4. Add the okra to the onion and stir for 1 minute or so before putting in the banana. Cook for 2 minutes over a high heat, adding more oil if required.
5. Now put in the lime or lemon juice and seasoning. Add enough water to generously cover the base of the pan. Cover and simmer for 15 minutes, adding more water or juice from time to time to give the desired consistency.
6. Five minutes before serving, put in the cooked rice to heat through ◆

Whole curd or yogurt curry

Serves 2-4

PREPARATION
5
MINUTES
25
COOKING

This curry can be served either with roti or with peas pilao. It has a great fresh taste.

Jaba Banerjee, Dhaka, Bangladesh

INGREDIENTS

- 1 pound / 450 g small whole potatoes
- 4-6 small whole onions
- 2 tomatoes
- 4 whole black peppercorns
- 3 cloves garlic
- 1/2 teaspoon fresh ginger, chopped
- 2 tablespoons yogurt or curd cheese
- 1/2 green chili, de-seeded and finely chopped
- pinch of sugar
- oil
- salt

1. First, boil the potatoes with the whole onions for 10 minutes; drain.
2. While they are cooking, heat the oil in a frying pan. Add peppercorns, ginger and garlic; stir it. Fry for a minute and then add a pinch of sugar.
3. Now put in the whole tomatoes and onions and fry for 3-4 minutes.
4. Pour in 1 cup/240 ml water and bring to the boil before adding the potatoes. Season with salt. Cook for 10 minutes or until there is just a little moisture left.
5. Now put the curd or yogurt into a cup, add a pinch of salt and 2 drops of oil. Mix well to make a smooth paste. Pour over the potato and tomato as a garnish, together with the green chili if using ◆

Mushroom and tofu stew

Vegan

Serves 2-3

PREPARATION 10 MINUTES

10 COOKING

This beancurd/tofu dish is a simple, soupy winter warmer, which would go well with plain boiled rice and stir-fried *bak choi* greens. Chinese cooking uses the more pungent variety of white pepper as a seasoning. If not available, black pepper may be used. If you can get your hands on mushroom soy sauce at a Chinese supermarket, buy a bottle. It has a lovely rich mushroomy flavor and can be used as a dip. For this dish, you could add a carrot cut into julienne sticks, and also a tablespoon of dry sherry. It helps to put out all the ingredients you will need before starting the recipe.

Dinyar Godrej, Rotterdam, Holland

INGREDIENTS

- 1/2 pound / 225 g mushrooms, sliced
- 1/4 pound / 110 g beancurd/tofu, diced
- 1 cup / 240 ml vegetable stock
- 2 tablespoons mushroom soy sauce or dark soy sauce
- 1 teaspoon sugar
- 1 tablespoon cornflour dissolved in a little cold water
- 1 teaspoon sesame oil
- 1 tablespoon sweet red chili sauce or 1 teaspoon mild red chili, de-seeded and thinly sliced
- 1-2 scallions/spring onions, finely chopped
- white pepper
- oil

1. To begin, mix the stock with the soy sauce and sugar.
2. Now pour some oil into a wok and on a high heat stir-fry the mushrooms for a minute. Drain on kitchen paper.
3. Add a little more oil and on a high heat fry the beancurd/tofu pieces for a minute.
4. Now return the mushrooms to the wok, add one of the scallions/spring onions, and then pour in the mixed stock, soy sauce and sugar. Bring to the boil and simmer for 2-3 minutes. Add the cornflour liquid and stir quickly.
5. Transfer to a warm serving dish and sprinkle on the sesame oil, chili sauce or chili and the other scallion/spring onion, before serving ◆

Preparing food near Beijing, China.
PHOTO: F. GREENE / HUTCHISON

Sweetcorn and snowpeas/mangetout

This is best served on its own, but if you want to make it more substantial by serving it cooked with noodles or rice, then double the quantity of soy sauce as they absorb the flavor. Or just serve the noodles separately.

Vegan

Serves 4

PREPARATION **5** MINUTES

10 COOKING

INGREDIENTS

- 1 cup / 150 g baby sweetcorn, sliced lengthwise
- ½ pound / 450 g snowpeas/mangetout
- ½ cup / 60 g cashew nuts
- 3 scallions/spring onions, chopped
- ½ teaspoon fresh ginger, finely chopped
- 1 tablespoon soy sauce
- oil
- salt

1. If using canned sweetcorn, drain first. If using fresh or frozen, cook in boiling water for a couple of minutes and then drain.
2. When ready, heat the oil in a wok to medium heat and then fry the cashews until golden. Remove, and drain on kitchen paper.
3. Now increase the heat and then toss in the sweetcorn and snowpeas/mangetout together with the ginger and scallions/spring onions. Sprinkle in the soy sauce and stir-fry briskly for 2 minutes.
4. Scatter the cashews on top and serve ◆

Mushroom sabzi

SAUTÉED MUSHROOMS

Vegan adaptable

Serves 2

PREPARATION
5
MINUTES
10
COOKING

Mushrooms are a delicacy in India and because of their relative rarity, they are often very simply treated when cooking, so that their flavor can be savored without drowning it in spices. This is a typical North Indian mushroom recipe.

INGREDIENTS

1/2 pound / 225 g mushrooms sliced

1 onion, thinly sliced *

1/2-1 green chili, de-seeded and thinly sliced

1/2 teaspoon fresh ginger, chopped

1/2 teaspoon garam masala

2 teaspoons lemon or lime juice

1 tablespoon fresh cilantro/coriander, chopped

ghee or oil

salt and pepper

* Red onion is best if possible.

1. Heat about 2 tablespoons of ghee or oil in a frying pan or wok and sauté the chili for half a minute. Add the sliced onion and continue to sauté for a further 3 minutes until the onion softens.
2. Now add the ginger and stir around for half a minute before adding the mushrooms. Stir-fry these over a high heat for a couple of minutes until done.
3. Just before switching off the heat, sprinkle on the garam masala and lemon or lime juice, and season. Stir, sprinkle with fresh cilantro/coriander and serve ◆

Khatti mithi masoor dal

SWEET AND SOUR RED LENTILS

Vegan adaptable

Serves 2-4

PREPARATION 5 MINUTES

15 COOKING

Khattoo, mithoo, tikhoo - sour, sweet and hot - this is the beloved combination of Indian Parsi cuisine, which positively revels in the use of rich ingredients. The Parsis, as the small community of Zoroastrians is called, came to India centuries ago from Persia at the time of the rise of Islam in their homelands. In India their customs as well as their cuisine underwent adaptations. Yet they have maintained their distinct identity and Parsi food is eagerly enjoyed by other Indians. This recipe does not belong to the heart-attack school of cooking typical of Parsi cuisine, but is a simple and lip-smacking variation on red lentils. It can easily be made in advance and reheats well.

Dinyar Godrej, Rotterdam, Holland

INGREDIENTS

- 1/2 pound / 225 g red lentils
- 8 cloves garlic
- 1-inch / 2.5-cm piece of fresh ginger
- 1-2 dried red chilis, de-seeded
- 1 1/2 teaspoons cumin seeds
- 1 1/2 teaspoons tamarind concentrate *
- 1 tablespoon dark brown sugar
- 1 1/2 cups / 400 ml water
- 3/4 teaspoon turmeric
- 2 tablespoons fresh cilantro/coriander, chopped
- ghee or oil
- salt

* Asian grocers sell tamarind in block or powdered form; follow packet instructions.

1. Place the lentils in a pan with the water and bring to the boil. Remove any froth that rises to the surface. Add the turmeric and salt and simmer for about 10 minutes.
2. While they are cooking, grind the garlic, ginger, chilis and cumin seeds to a paste with a mortar and pestle or in a coffee grinder.
3. Now heat a little ghee or oil in a small pan and add the ground spices. Fry, stirring, for 1 minute, adding a tablespoon of water if the paste starts to stick to the pan.
4. Add the spice paste to the pot with the lentils, along with the tamarind and sugar. Stir well and simmer for a further minute and then serve hot, sprinkled with the fresh cilantro/coriander ◆

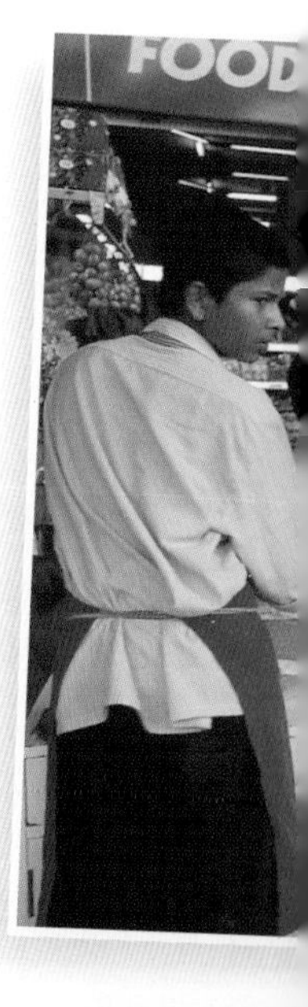

Chole

GARBANZO/CHICKPEA STEW

Vegan

Serves 3-4

PREPARATION **5** MINUTES **20** COOKING

Chickpeas or garbanzos are served up in many guises in different countries. In the Middle East they are popular in the dip, hummus, and in felafels, while in Latin America they feature in stews. This dish gives an exciting combination of flavors.

Gowri Rajendran, Gujerat, India

INGREDIENTS

- 1 cup / 150 g garbanzos/chickpeas, drained
- 1 onion, finely chopped
- 2 tomatoes, chopped
- 1/2 teaspoon chili powder
- 1/2 teaspoon garam masala
- 1/2 teaspoon turmeric
- 2 tablespoons fresh cilantro/coriander, chopped
- oil
- salt

1. Heat oil in a pan and fry the onions for 5 minutes. Then put in the tomatoes, chili powder, garam masala and turmeric, and stir-fry for 3 minutes.
2. After this, add the garbanzos/chickpeas, 1 tablespoon of the fresh cilantro/coriander, and salt.
3. Cook for 5-10 minutes, stirring, to combine the ingredients and flavors. Garnish with the remaining cilantro/coriander leaves and serve hot with bread or rice and raita ◆

Vegetable khichdi

This is a nutritious all-in-one meal. It is very popular in West and North India, and is usually prepared with just lentils and very little spice. In this recipe vegetables have been added to make it more exotic. You can vary the vegetables and use pretty much what you have to hand.

Lakshmi Menon, Mumbai, India

Vegan
Serves 4-6

PREPARATION **10** MINUTES

20 COOKING

INGREDIENTS

½ pound / 225 g rice
1 cup / 150 g red lentils
1 cup / 120 g peas
4 potatoes, diced
1 cup / 100 g cauliflower, finely chopped
2-4 onions, finely chopped
½ teaspoon cumin seeds
1-inch / 2.5-cm piece of cinnamon
3 cloves
3 cardamoms
1 teaspoon chili powder
½ teaspoon turmeric
oil
salt

1. Soak the lentils and rice in boiling water for 10 minutes. Drain.
2. While they are soaking, sauté the onions in a large saucepan for about 10 minutes until they are turning brown.
3. Now put in the rice, lentils, vegetables, cumin, cinnamon, cloves, cardamoms, chili powder and turmeric. Continue to fry until the rice sticks.
4. Pour in boiling water to cover, season and mix well. Cover, bring to the boil and then simmer on a low heat for 5-10 minutes until the rice, lentils and vegetables are cooked and the moisture is absorbed ◆

Aloo gobi mattar bhaji

POTATO, CAULIFLOWER AND PEA BHAJI

Vegan

Serves 4

PREPARATION 10 MINUTES

20 COOKING

Most North Indian dishes are cooked in oil, often a lot of it. Vegetables lose their flavor and nutrients when cooked for a long time in water, so this recipe uses just a little oil and then not too much water. Using the same method, other vegetables in season may be used such as carrots, cabbage, spinach and so on.

INGREDIENTS

1/2 pound / 225 g potatoes, diced
1/2 pound / 225 g cauliflower, cut small
1/2 pound / 225 g peas
1/2 teaspoon chili powder
1 teaspoon turmeric
1/2 teasoon garam masala
1/2 teaspoon cumin seeds
2 tablespoons fresh cilantro/coriander, chopped
oil
salt

1. First, heat the oil in saucepan and fry the chili powder, turmeric, garam masala and cumin seeds for 30 seconds-1 minute.
2. Then add the vegetables, half the cilantro/coriander leaves and salt, and stir-fry to mix the ingredients for 1 minute.
3. Pour in a little water to cover the base of the pan. Put on the lid and cook for 10-15 minutes, stirring from time to time and partially mashing the ingredients.
4. When cooked, garnish with the remaining cilantro/coriander leaves before serving ◆

Aloo-mattar

POTATO AND PEA CURRY

In this delicious recipe, the yogurt, tomatoes and cilantro/coriander give an intriguing flavor and the turmeric bestows a golden color.

Lakshmi Menon, Mumbai, India

Serves 2-4

PREPARATION

10

MINUTES

15

COOKING

INGREDIENTS

- 1 pound / 450 g potatoes, diced
- 1 cup / 120 g peas
- 1 onion chopped
- 1 teaspoon chili powder
- 2 teaspoons fresh ginger, chopped
- 1 teaspoon turmeric
- 1/2 teaspoon ground coriander
- 1 cup / 240 ml hot water
- 2-4 tomatoes, chopped
- 3 tablespoons yogurt
- 1 teaspoon garam masala
- 2 tablespoons fresh cilantro/coriander, chopped
- salt

1. Start by grinding or blending the onion with the chili powder and ginger to make a paste.
2. Now heat the oil in a saucepan and fry the blended paste for 1 minute before adding the turmeric and ground coriander. Continue to cook for 1-2 minutes, stirring.
3. Next, put in the potatoes, hot water and salt. Cover and boil for 3-5 minutes before adding the peas and tomatoes. Stir well and then continue to simmer, covered, for 5 minutes until most of the liquid has been absorbed. Remove from the heat.
4. When ready, blend the yogurt with a little water and add to the potato and pea sauce. Stir, and then sprinkle on the garam masala and fresh cilantro/coriander leaves ◆

Vegetables in coconut milk

Vegan

Serves 3

PREPARATION

15

MINUTES

20

COOKING

This is best made with fresh galangal if you can get it. Otherwise the dried or powdered version known as Laos powder will do. Despite the chili, this is a mild dish and you can use a range of vegetables such as egg-plant/aubergine, carrots, green beans, baby sweetcorn and beansprouts.

INGREDIENTS

1 pound / 450 g mixed vegetables sliced or chopped finely as necessary

1/2 red chili, de-seeded and sliced finely or 1/4 teaspoon chili powder

1/2 teaspoon fresh galangal, chopped or 1 teaspoon powdered *

2 stalks lemon grass, cut into 2-inch/5cm pieces *

1 cup / 240 ml coconut milk

oil

salt

* Available from speciality shops and Asian stores.

1. Heat some oil in the wok and put in the chili, lemon grass and galangal; stir well.
2. Now add the vegetables, beginning with those that will take longer to cook and adding the rest at intervals.
3. When the last of the vegetables are in, add the seasoning and pour in the coconut milk. Bring to the boil and then let simmer gently until the vegetables are done ◆

Watercress salad

This recipe is from the Luang Prabang in Laos where they grow a unique species of watercress (or so I was led to believe). Anyway, it's a great and very unusual summer salad. I've adapted it slightly - ie, no fish sauce - and I've used standard, supermarket watercress and lots of guessing... In Laos I ate this with sticky rice, but in Laos you eat everything with sticky rice! The dish is best prepared just before serving. At any rate, do not put the dressing on until the last minute, or the watercress and herbs may go limp. Omit the eggs for a vegan dish.

Gilly Wright, London

Vegan adaptable

Serves 2

INGREDIENTS

- ½ pound / 225 g watercress
- 2 tomatoes, quartered
- 5 inches / 12.5 cm cucumber, sliced
- 2 eggs
- 1 tablespoon fresh mint, chopped
- 1 tablespoon fresh cilantro/coriander, chopped
- 1 tablespoon peanuts, toasted under grill and chopped
- 2 tablespoons white wine vinegar
- 1 teaspoon sugar
- 2 teaspoons sesame oil
- 2 teaspoons soy sauce

1. First, put the eggs on to boil and cook for 8-10 minutes until they are hard. Then cool them, peel and chop into quarters.
2. In the meantime mix the watercress in a bowl with the tomatoes, cucumber and herbs.
3. Now dissolve the sugar in the white wine vinegar; add sesame oil and soy sauce and mix well.
4. Place the hard-cooked eggs around the top of the salad. Pile the nuts into the center and then pour over the dressing ◆

Nasi goreng

FRIED RICE

Serves 6

PREPARATION
10
MINUTES
30
COOKING

Rice dishes are very popular, and found at many food stalls around the country. At these, the tables and chairs are surrounded by the stalls where tasty meals are cooked up in a trice and brought to your table. You can take your pick from Malaysia's rich cuisines - Indian, Chinese or Malaysian (like this *nasi goreng*).

INGREDIENTS

1 pound / 450 g rice
6 eggs, beaten
1 onion, finely sliced
1 cup / 50 g beansprouts
1 cup / 150 g cabbage, thinly sliced
1 carrot, cut into thin sticks
3 sticks celery, finely sliced
4 scallions/spring onions, chopped
2 tablespoons soy sauce
oil
salt and pepper

1. First cook the rice by covering with boiling water. Cook for 10-15 minutes until just tender. Drain.
2. While the rice is boiling, heat the oil in a wok and sauté the onion for 3 minutes. Now put in the cabbage, carrot, celery, scallions/spring onions, and soy sauce. Stir-fry for a few more minutes.
3. Reduce the heat and add the rice to the vegetables in the wok and mix well. Season lightly and continue to cook gently, stirring from time to time.
4. Heat some more oil in a small pan, add the beaten eggs with a pinch of salt and scramble them quickly. When ready, add them to the rice and stir them in. Serve hot ◆

Noodles with basil

Access to a good local Chinese or Thai supermarket is a help for this recipe. It's a Thai noodle dish, the name of which completely escapes me at present. If you can, use Thai basil and not the tiny boxed greenery from a supermarket. Be cautious with the birds' eye chilis - amounts depend on how hot you can take your food. The authentic Thai version doubles as an incendiary device! Always check the ingredients on bean sauces as some have shrimp paste in them. This dish would go well with a simple stir-fry like *bak choi* greens. A splash of lemon gives it zing; lemon makes a good substitute for the ubiquitous fish sauce in many Thai dishes.

Gilly Wright, London

Vegan

Serves 2

PREPARATION **5** MINUTES **5** COOKING

INGREDIENTS

- 1/2 pound / 225 g flat rice noodles *
- 3 tablespoons of sweet basil, chopped
- 1-4 birds' eye chilis, halved and de-seeded
- 1 teaspoon sesame oil
- 1 teaspoon concentrated yellow bean sauce
- 1-2 tablespoons soy sauce
- 1/2 teaspoon sugar
- a little water
- oil

(yellow bean sauce, soy sauce, sugar and water: mixed together)

* Fresh rice noodles come oiled in bags and can just be added straight to a wok or dipped in hot water to separate out. Don't boil them though or they turn mushy. Dried rice noodles need to be soaked in hot but not boiling water for a minute or two to soften them.

1 Heat oil in a wok and fry the chilis for half a minute; this makes them less fiery.

2 Now add the noodles, thoroughly drained if they were placed in hot water, and fry for another minute or so. Add the sesame oil and 2 tablespoons of the basil.

3 Combine well and then add the yellow bean sauce and soy mixture and stir fry for about 1 minute, until it looks done. Remove and keep warm.

4 Heat a little more oil in the wok and fry the remaining basil which will go crispy in seconds. Sprinkle this over the top of the noodles ◆

Sweet and sour vegetables

Vegan

Serves 4

PREPARATION 10 MINUTES 10 COOKING

For this dish, you can generally use what vegetables you have around. Some good ones include thinly sliced carrot, cucumber, baby sweetcorn, snowpeas/mangetout, *bak choi* (Chinese cabbage), beansprouts, tomatoes, pineapple, bell peppers and mushrooms. It is best to make the sauce first.

Sarah Byham, Fukushima-ken, Japan

INGREDIENTS

1 pound / 450 g vegetables, finely chopped/sliced
1 cup / 150 g beancurd/tofu
1 onion, finely sliced
4 cloves garlic, crushed
1 red chili, de-seeded and sliced
oil

SAUCE

1 tablespoon lemon juice
3 tablespoons brown sugar
2 tablespoons soy sauce
3 tablespoons tomato sauce
2 tablespoons pineapple juice
½ teaspoon cornflour +

+ optional: see step 5

1 Mix all the ingredients for the sauce together and set aside.

2 Put some oil into a wok and when it is hot, stir-fry the onion until it begins to soften. Then add the garlic and stir-fry for a further minute.

3 Next, add the vegetables which take longer to cook such as carrots and bell peppers. Stir-fry these for 2-3 minutes.

4 Now put in the chili and rest of the vegetables, stirring until they are cooked.

5 Pour in the sauce and stir to combine well before serving. If you want a glossy sauce, add half a teaspoon of cornflour to the mixed sauce ingredients before pouring them into the wok ◆

Rau xao

STIR-FRIED VEGETABLES WITH BEANCURD/TOFU

After the rapprochement between the US and Vietnam in 1995, things have eased somewhat in the war-devastated country, but it remains one of the poorest in the world. The reform policies, known as *doi moi* (change to the new) aim to move Vietnam to a market economy which is unlikely to benefit the poorest people. This dish uses a range of vegetables and is fresh and crunchy with a variety of textures. If you have time, marinate the tofu first for a while (see step 1 below).

Vegan

Serves 2

PREPARATION
10
MINUTES

10
COOKING

INGREDIENTS

½ pound / 225 g beancurd/tofu, cubed
1 carrot, finely sliced
2 cups / 300 g broccoli, cut into small florets
1 green chili, de-seeded and sliced
1 cup / 50 g mushrooms, sliced
1 cup / 50 g beansprouts
3 scallions/spring onions, chopped
2 tablespoons soy sauce
2 cloves garlic, crushed
1 tablespoon lime or lemon juice
½ teaspoon ground ginger
½ teaspoon ground cumin
3 tablespoons fresh cilantro/coriander, chopped
oil

1. Combine the soy sauce with the garlic, lime or lemon juice, ginger and cumin and pour over the beancurd/tofu in a bowl. Set aside. This can be done some hours beforehand if desired.
2. Heat the oil in a wok and stir-fry the carrot for about 1 minute. Then add the broccoli and chili, if using, and cook, stirring, for another 2 minutes.
3. Next, add the mushrooms and the beancurd/tofu mixture. Stir-fry for 1-2 minutes and then add the beansprouts and scallions/spring onions. Stir-fry for half a minute and serve with the cilantro/coriander scattered on top ◆

Bean, cheese and tomato quesadillas

(PANCAKES)

Serves 4

PREPARATION
5
MINUTES
25
COOKING

Across most of South America, vegetarians can feel swamped by carnivores munching their way through quantities of beef and chicken. However there are plenty of dishes which give a tasty mix of beans, vegetables and peppers - and adding cheese as in this recipe gives an extra dimension.

INGREDIENTS

6 tortillas *

2 cups / 300 g red kidney beans, drained

3 tomatoes, chopped

1 green bell pepper, chopped

1 onion, finely sliced

2 cups / 225 g Monterey Jack or cheddar cheese, grated

1/2 teaspoon chili powder

1/2 teaspoon ground cumin

oil

salt and pepper

* Tortilla sizes can vary widely. This recipe assumes they are about 6 inches/12.5 cms in diameter, but if you can only find large ones then use two only and slice them into two, to feed 4, or make more filling.

Heat oven to 375°F/190°C/Gas 5

1. Start by heating the oil and gently cooking the onion for 5 minutes. Then put in the tomatoes and bell pepper, the chili powder and cumin, salt and pepper and continue to cook for 5 minutes, stirring frequently.

2. Now put in the beans and heat them through. Partially mash them with a fork, and mix all the ingredients well together.

3. Spoon some of the mixture on each prepared tortilla, and roll up. Put any remaining mixture around the tortillas in a lightly greased baking dish.

4. Scatter the cheese on top and bake for 10-15 minutes until the cheese has melted ◆

Sweetcorn and bean casserole

Corn and beans are two classic staples of Central America. As well as complementing each other nutritionally, the two plants are commonly grown together as the bean plants capture or 'fix' nitrogen from the air and release it into the soil to nourish the maize/corn. If using canned beans and sweetcorn, keep the liquid for step 2 below, or else use stock or water.

Vegan

Serves 4

PREPARATION **5** MINUTES **25** COOKING

INGREDIENTS

- 1 cup / 150 g sweetcorn
- 1 cup / 150 g red kidney beans
- 2 cups / 400 g canned tomatoes or 4-6 fresh tomatoes, chopped
- 1 onion, finely chopped
- 2 cloves garlic, crushed
- 1 green bell pepper, finely chopped +
- 1/4 -1/2 teaspoon chili powder
- 1/2 teaspoon ground ginger
- 1/2 teaspoon ground cumin
- oil
- salt

+ optional

1. First heat the oil and sauté the onion for 10 minutes before adding the garlic, the chili powder, ginger and cumin. Continue to cook for 2 minutes, stirring.
2. Now put in the tomatoes, bell pepper if using, sweetcorn and beans. Add some of the retained bean or sweetcorn liquid (or water/stock) as desired. Season with salt.
3. Cover the pan and cook gently for 10 minutes. Partially mash the mixture, and cook for a further 5 minutes before serving with bread, rice or potatoes and salad ◆

Empanadas

TURNOVERS

Vegan adaptable

Serves 4

PREPARATION
10
MINUTES
30
COOKING

Unlike Brazilian cooking which shows both African and indigenous Indian influence, Chile along with Argentina and Uruguay has mainly European cuisine. The former Spanish colonies reveal some Arabic traces too, as in this recipe with its use of nuts and dried fruit.

These turnovers are tasty and easy to do; they are also good eaten cold. They would usually be made with maize flour, but this recipe substitutes shop-bought puff pastry. They are vegan adaptable if you omit the egg and use vegan pastry.

INGREDIENTS

- ½ pound / 225 g frozen puff pastry, thawed
- 2 eggs
- 1 onion, finely chopped
- 1 red bell pepper, finely chopped
- ½ cup / 60 g pine nuts or chopped walnuts
- 1 tablespoon sultanas or raisins
- ¼ teaspoon chili powder
- oil
- salt and pepper

Heat oven to 400°F/200°C/Gas 6

1. If using them, first set the eggs to cook in boiling water until they are hard. Drain, cool and then remove shells and chop finely.
2. While that is going on, heat the oil and sauté the onion for a few minutes before adding the bell pepper, nuts, sultanas or raisins, chili powder, salt and pepper. Simmer for 10 minutes and then put in the chopped egg. Mix well.
3. Roll out the pastry to a ⅛-inch/2-mm thickness and then cut it into circles using a saucer.
4. Place a spoonful of the mix on one half of the pastry circle and fold over the other side. Press the edge with a fork to seal and prick to allow steam release. Repeat until all the pastry and mixture are finished.
5. Place on a baking tray lined with baking paper or dusted with flour and bake for 10 minutes until golden. You may want to turn them over halfway through to let the undersides brown as well ◆

Locro

PUMPKIN STEW

Serves 4-5

PREPARATION
15
MINUTES

20
COOKING

Like its neighbors Colombia and Peru, Ecuador was once part of the sprawling Inca empire, and as well as sharing this history it has similar geography dominated by the Andes mountains. Ecuador's version of the South America *seviche* - fish soaked in lime juice - is famous, and *locro* is another well-liked meal, made with potatoes and cheese, and here with the addition of sweetcorn and pumpkin. This is a good homely stew, with the kinds of uncomplicated flavors that often go down well with the kids.

INGREDIENTS

1 cup / 150 g sweetcorn
1 pound / 450 g pumpkin, cut into small pieces
1/2 cup / 60 g frozen or fresh peas
4 potatoes, diced
1 onion, finely chopped
2 cloves garlic, crushed
2 tablespoons tomato paste
1/2 pound / 225 g cheese, grated
1/2-1 teaspoon nutmeg
oil
salt and pepper

1. Start by boiling or steaming the pumpkin pieces for 10-15 minutes until soft. Drain and mash.
2. While the pumpkin is cooking, heat the oil and gently fry the onion, adding the garlic after 5 minutes. Stir.
3. Now put in the tomato paste and potatoes, adding enough water to just cover the potatoes. Boil for 5 minutes before adding the corn, pumpkin and peas.
4. Now turn the heat right down, cover the pan and cook for 10 minutes. Scatter the grated cheese and nutmeg on top before serving with a salad ◆

Potato and cabbage fields, Ecuador.
PHOTO: JEREMY HORNER / HUTCHISON

Pumpkin curry

I travel frequently to Guyana, and this curry made by a friend, Sharron Thomas, is always a welcoming meal. We often have it with prawns, but if you want to omit them that is fine. Preparing the pumpkin is quite time-consuming, and it helps to have a really strong sharp knife for this.

Dig Woodvine, UK

Vegan adaptable

Serves 2-4

PREPARATION **10** MINUTES **25** COOKING

INGREDIENTS

- 1 1/2 pounds / 600 g pumpkin, cut into cubes
- 1/4 pound / 110 g prawns +
- 1 onion, finely chopped
- 2 cloves garlic, finely chopped
- 1/2 chili, de-seeded and finely chopped
- 1/2 teaspoon brown sugar
- oil
- salt

+ optional

1. Start by cooking the pumpkin cubes in boiling water for 10-15 minutes or until almost cooked. Drain.
2. While that is happening, heat the oil in a frying pan, and sauté the onion for 8-10 minutes before adding the garlic and chili. Stir, and cook these ingredients gently for a further 5 minutes.
3. Now put in the cubes of pumpkin, and prawns if using, and allow to simmer down for 10 minutes until the mixture looks dry. Add sugar and salt to taste. Serve with fresh puri or pitta bread ◆

Rice and peas

Vegan

Serves 4

PREPARATION 5 MINUTES

20 COOKING

Although the Caribbean islands share many dishes, such as the rice and peas one here, Jamaica has one dish that did not really spread elsewhere. This is is akee with saltfish (cod) or with shrimp. Akee, which grows on a handsome tree, is a red fruit eaten for its scrambled-egg flavored pulp. It was introduced to Jamaica by Captain Bligh (of Mutiny on the Bounty fame) from West Africa in 1793.

INGREDIENTS

1/2 pound / 225 g rice

1 cup / 150 g red peas* or kidney beans

1 onion, finely sliced

1 clove garlic, crushed

1/2 red chili, de-seeded and finely chopped +

1 cup / 240 ml coconut milk

a few drops Tabasco or pepper sauce or 1/4 teaspoon chili powder

oil

salt and pepper

* Red peas are the ones inside haricot beans.

+ optional

1 To begin, boil the rice for 10 minutes or according to packet instructions until it is almost ready.

2 While that is going on, heat the oil and fry the onion for 10 minutes before adding the garlic and chili if using. Cook together for 2 minutes and then add the peas or beans, the coconut milk and salt and pepper. Mix well.

3 Add the drained, cooked rice and combine well. Continue to cook for 10 minutes until the rice is soft, the flavors expanded, and most of the liquid absorbed. Then serve with the Tabasco/pepper sauce or chili powder sprinkled over ◆

Zucchini/courgette and sweetcorn stew

Vegan

Serves 2-3

PREPARATION 10 MINUTES

15 COOKING

Formerly home of the Aztec and other indians, then a Spanish colony, Mexico's cultural mix is visible today in the colorful indian markets nestling beside elegant colonial churches. High-rise buildings mark today's industrial Mexico - as do the *maquilas* (cheap labor factories) lining the border with the US.

Many of the most familiar beans - like kidney beans - originated in the Americas. They are nearly always served in some form or other at mealtimes, and make a nourishing contribution for vegetarians. See below the recipe for a good way to use up any left-overs.

INGREDIENTS

- 1 pound / 450 g zucchini/courgettes, finely sliced
- 1 cup / 150 g sweetcorn, drained
- 1 cup / 150 g red kidney beans, drained
- 1 red bell pepper, chopped
- 1 onion, finely chopped
- 2 cloves garlic, crushed
- 1/2 teaspoon chili powder
- oil
- salt and pepper

1. Heat the oil in a large pan or wok and sauté the onion for 5-10 minutes until it softens. Then put in the garlic, red bell pepper, slices of zucchini/courgette and chili powder, and continue to cook together for 5 minutes, stirring to mash the ingredients a little.
2. Now put in the sweetcorn and beans. Stir and season.
3. Cover the wok or pan and simmer the stew for 10-15 minutes. Any remainders can be reheated, mashed and served in tacos (see below).

Taco shells

Heat oven to 380°F/180°C/Gas 4

1. Put the taco shells on a baking sheet and heat through in the oven for 5 minutes.
2. Remove from the oven and fill the taco shells with the stuffing. Serve hot with salad ◆

Spiced lentil stew

Vegan

Serves 4-6

PREPARATION
10
MINUTES
20
COOKING

Everyday food for many North Africans will often feature soups based on beans or lentils and vegetables. *Tagines* are also widespread; these are stews cooked slowly in an earthenware pot over a charcoal fire or slow heat, and mopped up with once-risen bread (*khobz*). Vegans should omit the yogurt in step 4.

INGREDIENTS

- 1/2 pound / 225 g red lentils
- 1 onion, finely sliced
- 3/4 teaspoon turmeric
- 2 tomatoes, chopped
- 2 cloves garlic, crushed
- 1 teaspoon ground cumin
- 1 teaspoon ground ginger
- 1/4 teaspoon cinnamon
- 1/4 teaspoon chili powder
- 2 tablespoons fresh cilantro/coriander, chopped
- 1 tablespoon oil
- salt and pepper

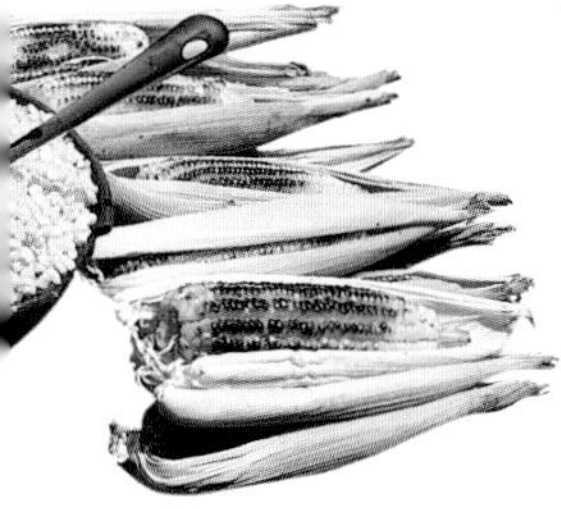

1. First, put the lentils in a saucepan with half the onion and the turmeric. Pour boiling water over to cover, bring to the boil and then simmer for 15 minutes until the lentils are almost cooked and most of the water gone.
2. While the lentils are cooking, heat the oil in a saucepan large enough to take the lentils later on, and sauté the other half of the onion for 5 minutes.
3. Then add the garlic, cumin, ginger, cinnamon and chili powder and stir round to cook for 1-2 minutes. Add the tomatoes now and mix them in.
4. When the lentils are ready, spoon them into the fried ingredients and stir well to mix. Season. Scatter in the cilantro/coriander, stir, and then simmer for 2-3 minutes before serving with hot pitta bread and yogurt ◆

Shourabat adas

LENTIL SOUP-STEW

This is one of the classic stews of the region, and its mix of lentils, garbanzos/chickpeas and bulgur with vegetables makes it tasty as well as nutritious. To make this into more of soup than a stew, double the quantity of stock. It has a nice nutty texture, and the tomato makes a splash of red against the pale pulses and green parsley.

Vegan

Serves 4-6

PREPARATION
10
MINUTES

COOKING

INGREDIENTS

- 1/2 cup / 110 g red lentils
- 1 cup / 150 g garbanzos/chickpeas, drained (keep liquid)
- 1/2 cup / 110 g bulgur
- 1 tomato, chopped
- 1 stick celery, finely sliced
- 1 carrot, thinly sliced
- 1 onion, chopped
- 1 clove garlic, chopped
- 1 teaspoon ground cumin
- 1 teaspoon ground coriander
- 2 1/2 cups / 600 ml stock
- 2 tablespoons fresh parsley, chopped
- oil
- salt and pepper

1. Start by soaking the red lentils in boiling water for 10 minutes. Drain.
2. While they are soaking, heat the oil in a saucepan and cook the onion for 10 minutes. Then put in the garlic, cumin, coriander and half the parsley. Cook these for 2 minutes.
3. Now add the tomato, celery and carrot and continue to fry these for 5 minutes.
4. After this, put in the drained lentils and bulgur. Pour in the stock, cover, and simmer for 10 minutes. Season, and then spoon in the garbanzos/chickpeas. Mix well, and continue to cook for 10-15 minutes. If you require more liquid, use a little of the retained chickpea juice. Serve with the remaining parsley on top ◆

Garbanzo/chickpea and tomato stew

Vegan

Serves 4-6

PREPARATION

5

MINUTES

20

COOKING

My parents emigrated from Syria to Canada in the 1920s, bringing with them their heritage of regional food. Hardy legumes such as broad beans, garbanzos/chickpeas, lentils and other common vegetables which thrive in semi-arid lands kept people in the Middle East well-fed and healthy. Fresh from our hand-watered garden in summer and dried in winter, they were prepared with herbs and spices, becoming the sustenance of our lives.

Habeeb Salloum/Vegetarian Resource Group

INGREDIENTS

1 cup / 150 g garbanzos/chickpeas
¼ cup / 40 g rice
1 onion, finely chopped
2 cloves garlic, crushed
1 cup / 240 ml tomato juice or canned tomatoes, chopped
1 teaspoon allspice
¼ teaspoon chili powder
2 tablespoons fresh cilantro/coriander, chopped
oil
salt and pepper

1 To begin, boil the rice for 5-10 minutes until it is still crunchy but almost cooked. Drain.

2 Meanwhile, heat the oil in a saucepan and gently fry the onion for 8-10 minutes. Then add the garlic, allspice and chili powder and cook for a further minute, stirring all the time.

3 Next, put in the garbanzos/chickpeas, rice, tomato juice or tomatoes, cilantro/coriander and seasoning. Mix well and then cover and simmer over a medium heat for 10 minutes to complete the rice cooking and let the flavors mingle, stirring frequently ◆

Stuffed zucchini/courgettes

Zucchini or courgettes are the variety of marrow that have been devloped to be cut when small. The marrow family which is related to cucmbers and melons, includes squashes, pumpkins and also *chayote* - a pear-shaped marrow popular in Central American cookery.

Serves 2-4

PREPARATION
10
MINUTES

INGREDIENTS

- 4 zucchini/courgettes, sliced in half lengthwise
- 1-2 onions, finely sliced
- 2 cloves garlic, crushed
- 2 tablespoons pine nuts +
- ½ teaspoon ground cumin
- ½ pound / 225 g Monterey Jack or cheddar cheese, grated
- 2 tablespoons fresh parsley or cilantro/coriander, chopped
- pinch of chili powder or a few drops of chili sauce +
- oil
- salt and pepper

+ optional

Heat oven to 400°F/200°C/Gas 6, or light the grill

1. First, parboil the sliced zucchini/courgettes for 5-8 minutes and then cool under cold water. When cool enough to handle, scoop out the pulp and chop it finely. Keep the zucchini/courgette shells.
2. While the zucchini/courgettes are cooking, heat the oil and sauté the onion for 5 minutes. Then put in the garlic, pine nuts if using, the cumin, 1 tablespoon of the parsley or cilantro/coriander, and seasoning. Cook for 1 minute.
3. Now add the chopped zucchini/courgette pulp to the onion mix and cook for 10 minutes, stirring.
4. While that is cooking, lightly grease a baking dish and then lay the zucchini/courgette shells in it. Pile on the mixture, put the grated cheese on top and cook in the oven, or under the grill, for 5-10 minutes. Scatter the remaining herbs on top before serving ◆

Couscous

Vegan

Serves 4

PREPARATION 10 MINUTES

25 COOKING

Couscous is today eaten throughout the Arab world and in many other places as well. It is a national dish in the Maghreb countries of Morocco, Algeria and Tunisia but each country has its special treatment. The Moroccans often put in saffron to impart a subtle aroma; Algerians may emphasize the taste of tomatoes while in Tunisia the couscous may be spiced up with ginger and chilis. Often the dish is accompanied by the region's fiery condiment, *harissa*. *Couscous* itself is a fine semolina grain (made from wheat) which is usually cooked by steaming it above the vegetables. If you do not have a *couscousier* (special pan) you can use a sieve placed above (but not in) the cooking vegetables.

INGREDIENTS

1/2 pound / 225 g couscous
2 onions, finely chopped
1/2 cup / 75 g garbanzos/chickpeas
1/2 cup / 75 g broad beans
2 tomatoes, chopped
2 carrots, sliced
1 green bell pepper or turnip, finely chopped
1 zucchini/courgette, sliced
1 tablespoon raisins or sultanas
1/4 teaspoon saffron or turmeric *
2 tablespoons fresh parsley, chopped
2 tablespoons fresh cilantro/coriander, chopped
1/2 teaspoon chili powder
1 teaspoon paprika
1 tablespoon margarine
oil
salt and pepper

* Turmeric does not have the same flavor as saffron but it does yield a similar yellow color.

1 First, heat the oil in a saucepan large enough to take the other ingredients (and one in which your sieve, if using, will sit comfortably). Fry the onions until soft.

2 Now put in all the other ingredients, except the couscous, and season well. Stir to combine.

3 Next, pour over just enough boiling water to cover. Place the couscous in the sieve or *couscousier* and suspend above the vegetables. Put the lid on the saucepan, bring to the boil and then simmer for 10-15 minutes until everything is ready. Spoon out the couscous onto a large plate, or onto individual plates, and then pile the vegetables on top ◆

TUNISIA

Chakchouka

VEGETABLE OMELET

Tunisia is a popular holiday destination for sun-starved northern Europeans, and currently it receives roughly double the number of tourists as neighboring Morocco. Similar to the region's *eggeh* dishes which are served hot or cold, this omelet is a tasty addition to the quick repertoire.

Serves 4-6

INGREDIENTS

6 eggs
4 tablespoons milk
1 onion, finely sliced
1/2 green bell pepper, finely sliced
4 tomatoes, chopped
1/2 teaspoon ground cumin
1 teaspoon ground coriander
oil
salt

1. Sauté the onion in the oil until it turns golden. Then put in the bell pepper and fry that for 2 minutes before adding the tomatoes, cumin, coriander and salt. Cook over a gentle heat for 10 minutes.
2. Beat the eggs and add the milk. Raise the heat and pour the eggs over the vegetables. Let the omelet cook to brown the base for 2 minutes.
3. Heat the grill and then brown the top side for a few minutes before serving ◆

Salads & Side Dishes

Making fufu (pounded yam) Accra, Ghana.

PHOTO: LIBA TAYLOR / HUTCHISON

GHANA

Spinach and tomato stew

'The cattle are healthy, their udders are full
And they might even smile at milking
Especially now that their milk and their meat go to
far away places to feed
mouths that are less
hungry than our own.'

Vegan

Serves 2-4

PREPARATION **5** MINUTES **20** COOKING

So writes Ghanaian poet Ama Ata Aidoo in *For Kinna II*, lamenting Ghana's dependence on exports. This is a sour relish to go with rice or potatoes. If using frozen spinach, you do not need to let it thaw - but allow a little extra cooking time. The mixture will be wetter.

INGREDIENTS

1 pound / 450 g spinach, chopped
1 onion, finely sliced
3 tomatoes, chopped
1 tablespoon tomato paste
1/2 teaspoon chili powder or paprika
1 tablespoon peanuts, chopped
oil
salt

1. Heat the oil in a pan and sauté the onion for 5-8 minutes. When it begins to turn golden, add the tomatoes and tomato paste and mix well.
2. Next, put in the spinach, chili or paprika and seasoning. Cover and cook for 10 minutes or so, until the spinach is cooked. Scatter the chopped peanuts on top before serving ◆

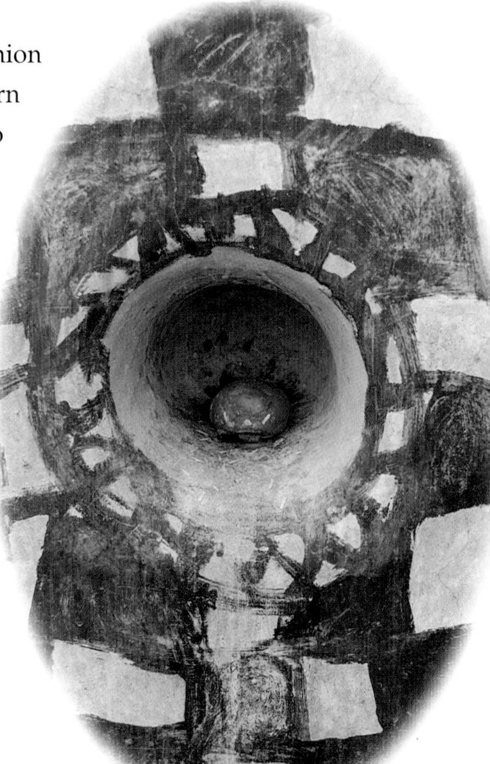

Sweetcorn and tomatoes

Vegan

Serves 3-4

PREPARATION 5 MINUTES

20 COOKING

Kenya's cuisine largely revolves around meat, and even poor families who do not often get to eat it themselves will try and provide *nyama choma* (roast meat) for guests. For vegetarians there are plenty of beans, sweetcorn and egg dishes but these will not probably appear on restaurant menus – so ask! The lemon gives this recipe a bright flavor, making for a tangy side dish.

INGREDIENTS

2 cups / 300 g sweetcorn *
6 tomatoes, chopped
6 curry leaves +
1/2 teaspoon chili powder
1/2 teaspoon mustard seeds
1 teaspoon ground cumin
3 tablespoons fresh cilantro/coriander, chopped
juice of 1 lemon
oil
salt

* If using frozen, cook according to packet instructions. If using canned, drain.

\+ optional

1. Heat the oil and cook the tomatoes together with the curry leaves, if using, the chili, mustard seeds, cumin, cilantro/coriander, lemon juice and salt.
2. Cover, and simmer for 10 minutes before adding the sweetcorn. Stir well and then cook for 5-10 more minutes to let the flavors combine ◆

Sweet potatoes with tomatoes

Sweet potatoes are versatile and quick to cook. This version brings out their sweetness, and the tomatoes and chili make a pleasantly tart counterpoint.

Vegan

Serves 2

PREPARATION 5 MINUTES

15 COOKING

INGREDIENTS

- 2 sweet potatoes, peeled and sliced into rounds ½-inch/1-cm thick
- 3 tomatoes, sliced
- ¼ teaspoon chili powder
- oil
- salt

1. Boil the slices of sweet potato for 5-10 minutes until almost cooked. Drain.
2. Heat the oil in a pan and fry the sweet potato pieces in hot oil, turning, until they are brown on both sides; season.
3. Arrange the tomatoes on top and serve immediately, with the chili powder and salt sprinkled over ◆

Cabbage casserole

Vegan

Serves 3-4

PREPARATION

10

MINUTES

25

COOKING

Lesotho, encircled by South Africa, has had four coups d'état since independence in 1964, something current King Letsie III (crowned in 1997) no doubt hopes to avoid. Wool and mohair are two of the main exports of the mountainous kingdom. This straightforward cabbage dish is also good cold.

INGREDIENTS

- 1 pound / 450 g cabbage, chopped finely
- 1 onion, finely chopped
- 3 tomatoes, chopped
- 1/2-1 teaspoon curry powder
- oil
- salt

1. Start by frying the onion in the oil for 10 minutes or until it is soft. Then add the curry powder and salt; stir well to distribute.
2. Next, put in the cabbage and a little water, stirring. Cover the pan and boil for 10 minutes or until the cabbage is cooked.
3. Add the tomatoes now, stir well, and cook for 5 minutes before serving ◆

Yellow rice

Falling prices for tea - one of Malawi's main exports - have dealt the economy a severe blow. Malawi is the second largest tea producer in Africa after Kenya. Most of the bushes are over 30 years old, but as a new bush takes up to 5 years before yielding bountifully, smallholder farmers are wary of digging up the old bushes. Rice is now common in Malawi alongside old mainstays, maize and sorghum.

Vegan

Serves 2

PREPARATION **5** MINUTES

15 COOKING

INGREDIENTS

1 cup / 150 g rice

1 cup / 100 g sultanas or raisins

1 teaspoon turmeric

1 stick cinnamon

salt

1 Cover the rice with boiling water, and then add the other ingredients; stir.

2 Now bring to the boil, and cook for 10 minutes or according to packet instructions until the rice is cooked and the water absorbed. Drain if necessary ◆

Coconut rice

Vegan
Serves 4-6

PREPARATION
5
MINUTES
20
COOKING

Frelimo, the former guerilla movement, maintains its rule in Mozambique despite the attempts of the opposition Renamo to bring it down. Partly as a result of the long civil war, the country remains one of the poorest in the world, exporting prawns, fish, cotton and cashew nuts to try and balance the books. This simple dish has a lovely pink color and a pleasant consistency.

INGREDIENTS

- 2 cups / 300 g rice
- 1 onion, finely chopped
- 1 1/2 cups / 360 ml coconut milk
- 2 tomatoes, chopped
- 1/2 green chili, de-seeded and finely sliced, or 1/4 teaspoon chili powder
- oil
- salt

1. To begin, boil the rice for 10-15 minutes or according to packet instructions, until it is just ready. Drain.
2. While it is cooking, heat the oil and gently cook the onion, adding the chili or chili powder when the onion begins to soften after 5 minutes or so.
3. Now put in the tomatoes and coconut milk, and simmer for 5 minutes, stirring from time to time.
4. Transfer the rice to the pan with the tomatoes and coconut milk and cook together gently for 5-10 minutes, stirring to combine well ◆

Tomato salad

Vegan

Serves 2-4

PREPARATION

5

MINUTES

0

COOKING

The name Sierra Leone suggests that a lion-shaped mountain must lie somewhere in this West African land, but this is not the case. The name probably arose from the many lions roaming there in the 15th century when the Europeans first made landfall.

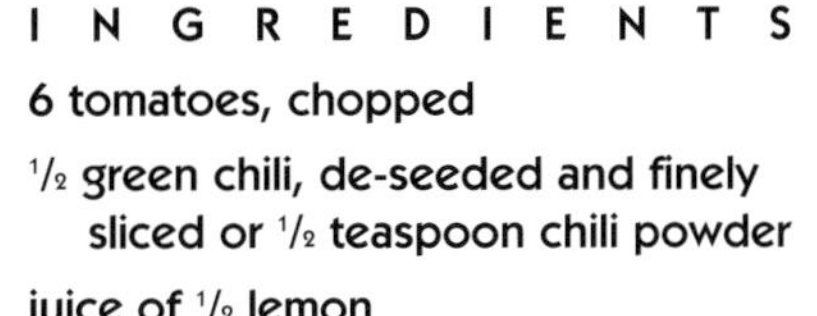

INGREDIENTS

6 tomatoes, chopped

½ green chili, de-seeded and finely sliced or ½ teaspoon chili powder

juice of ½ lemon

salt

1 Put the tomatoes in a salad bowl. Mix all other ingredients together and pour over the tomatoes ◆

Tuareg cooking pots, Mali.
PHOTO: MARY JELLIFFE / HUTCHISON

Spicy potatoes

'At the World Bank they asked me "How did you fail?" I responded: In 1988, Tanzania's per-capita income was $280. Now, in 1998, it is $140. Yet in those ten years Tanzania has done everything the IMF and World Bank wanted. So I asked the World Bank people: "What went wrong?" '

Julius Nyerere, first President of Tanzania

Vegan

Serves 2-4

PREPARATION **10** MINUTES

30 COOKING

INGREDIENTS

½ pound / 225 g potatoes, diced
1 onion, finely chopped
2 cloves garlic, crushed
2 teaspoons tomato paste
2 tablespoons lemon juice
1 teaspoon turmeric
½ teaspoon coriander seeds
¼ teaspoon cinnamon
pinch of chili powder
1 tablespoon fresh parsley or cilantro/coriander, chopped
oil
salt

1 First, parboil the potatoes for 5-10 minutes and then drain them.

2 While they are cooking, heat the oil in a frying pan or wok and sauté the onion for 5-8 minutes before adding the garlic. Stir and cook for 2-3 minutes.

3 Now put in the chopped potatoes, tomato paste, lemon juice, turmeric, and other ingredients. Mix well, and then pour in enough water to cover the base of the pan.

4 Cover the pan and cook for 10 minutes or so, stirring from time to time, until the potatoes are cooked, and the liquid mostly absorbed ◆

Spinach in coconut milk

Vegan
Serves 4

PREPARATION
5
MINUTES
20
COOKING

This dish has a creamy, pleasant flavor. You can use canned or frozen spinach, but drain it well.

INGREDIENTS

2 pounds / 900 g spinach, chopped
1 onion, finely chopped
1 cup / 240 ml coconut milk
1 cup / 200 g canned tomatoes, chopped
1 teaspoon curry powder
salt

1. Put the onion and tomatoes into a pan and bring to the boil; cook for 5 minutes.
2. When ready, add the spinach, and pour in the coconut milk.
3. Bring to the boil and simmer gently for 10-15 minutes, stirring frequently, until all the ingredients are cooked. Serve with other dishes, or with rice ◆

Tomato raita

Most of the 'Indian' restaurants in the UK are in fact Bangladeshi. Despite that country's current image, it was once a rich and fertile land. So what happened? One contributory factor could be British rule for 190 years... This raita is delicious with a fresh tangy taste.

Serves 4-6

PREPARATION **10** MINUTES

0 COOKING

INGREDIENTS

- 2 cups / 440 ml yogurt
- 2 tomatoes, finely chopped
- 2 cloves, crushed
- seeds from 2 cardamoms, crushed
- ½ teaspoon ground cumin
- ¼ teaspoon chili powder
- salt

1 Mix everything together in a bowl and serve as a relish or snack ◆

Stir-fried noodles with bamboo shoots and mushrooms

Serves 4

PREPARATION
10
MINUTES
5
COOKING

This is a good noodle side-dish - the bamboo shoots and ginger lift it above similar dishes. The mix of ginger and lemon gives this a good zesty flavor.

INGREDIENTS

1/2 pound / 225 g egg noodles
1/2 cup / 100 g canned bamboo shoots, drained
8 mushrooms, sliced
1 cup / 50 g beansprouts
2 tablespoons soy sauce
1 tablespoon rice wine or sherry
1/2 inch / 1 cm fresh ginger, finely chopped or 1 teaspoon ground ginger
lemon juice
oil
salt

1 Cook the egg noodles as instructed on the packet. Drain.

2 Heat the oil in a wok and stir-fry the bamboo shoots and mushrooms with the ginger for 1 minute before adding the beansprouts. Stir-fry these for 30 seconds.

3 Now put in the soy sauce, rice wine or sherry, salt and the noodles. Stir well to mix all the ingredients, add lemon juice to taste, and serve hot ◆

Upma

SEMOLINA WITH MUSTARD SEEDS

When you see this dish, which uses semolina (*rava*), it looks rather like mashed potato. But on tasting it, you'll find an interesting mixture of the bland and the spicy. The white *urad* dal - commonly used in *dosa* (rice pancakes) - contribute both to the flavor and also a pleasant crunchiness. A more substantial version can be made by adding finely-cut carrots, peas, and french beans. This is also a popular South Indian dish, especially for lighter meals or at teatime.

Gowri Rajendran, Gujerat, India

Vegan

Serves 2-4

INGREDIENTS

1 cup / 150 g semolina
1½ cups / 350 ml water
1 teaspoon mustard seeds
2 teaspoons urad dal
1 dried red chili, de-seeded and finely chopped
1 tablespoon fresh cilantro/coriander, chopped
1 tablespoon grated or desiccated coconut +
salt
oil

+ optional

1 Start by soaking the urad dal in boiling water for 5 minutes, and then drain them well.

2 Now pour a bit of oil in a frying pan and add the mustard seeds, urad dal and chili to the oil. When the mustard seeds splutter, remove from the heat and then carefully pour in the water.

3 Return the pan to the heat and as the water boils, pour in the semolina slowly while stirring vigorously. Add the salt, half the cilantro/coriander and coconut and mix these in well.

4 Continue to stir for a few minutes until the semolina has cooked and the water evaporated.

5 Garnish with the remaining cilantro/coriander leaves and grated coconut, if using. Serve hot ◆

Jeera and kalonji rice

RICE WITH CUMIN AND ONION SEEDS

Vegan

Serves 2-3

PREPARATION 5 MINUTES 15 COOKING

This simple dish makes a pleasant variation to plain boiled rice. And in saying 'plain boiled rice' it is easy to forget that this grain is the main staple food for around half the world's population, and its production involves over one billion people. Onion seeds are often sold as *kalonji* or *nigella*.

INGREDIENTS

½ pound / 225 g rice
1 onion, sliced into thin rings
1 teaspoon onion seeds
1 teaspoon cumin seeds
oil
salt

1. First heat the oil in a saucepan and fry the onion rings until brown. Remove them and set aside.
2. Using the same pan, fry the cumin and onion seeds for 2-3 minutes.
3. When that is done, put in the rice and stir it round. Then cover with boiling water and cook for 10-15 minutes until the water has been absorbed. Serve the rice with the onion rings on top ◆

Puri

BREAD

Puris - little puffed breads - should be eaten hot and so must be cooked just a few minutes before eating. For best results, roll them very flat. Most puri recipes include oil in the dough as well, because this helps the puris to fluff up when they are later fried. The heat of the oil combining with the water turning into steam makes them balloon out. Even if they do not look as good as your local Indian restaurant, it is worth perservering as they are very quick to do, and delicious with many meals. The wholewheat flour - *atta* - used in Indian kitchens is more finely ground than the flour sold in Western shops and supermarkets, and if you have an Asian grocery store nearby it is worth buying a pack.

Lakshmi Menon, Mumbai, India

Vegan

Makes 10-12

PREPARATION **15** MINUTES

1-2 each COOKING

INGREDIENTS

2 cups / 250 g flour or *atta*

8 tablespoons water

oil

salt

1 First knead together the flour, salt and two tablespoons of oil with water to make a stiff but pliable dough. Keep aside for 5-10 minutes, wrapped in or covered by a damp cloth.

2 When ready, roll out walnut-sized balls of the dough into very flat, even circles of about 3-inches/7.5-cms in diameter.

3 Heat the oil in a pan or wok and fry the puris, one at a time for 1-2 minutes until they puff up and are lightly brown. The best results are achieved by pushing the puri down in the hot oil with a long-handled metal spoon until it starts to fluff up and then releasing it. Remember to turn them once in the oil so both sides cook evenly.

4 Drain on kitchen paper, and serve hot to accompany snacks or main dishes ◆

Beansprout salad

Vegan

Serves 2-4

PREPARATION
5
MINUTES

0
COOKING

This refreshing salad, from Maharashtra and Gujarat, uses sprouted beans such as mung, or alfafa. Ingredients can vary to include tomatoes, beetroots, radish, pineapple, pomegranate seeds, cooked green peas or french beans.

INGREDIENTS

1 carrot

2 inches / 12.5 cms cucumber

½ cup / 25 g beansprouts

1 scallion/spring onion, finely sliced +

juice of 1 lime

1 tablespoon fresh cilantro/coriander, finely chopped

salt and pepper

+ optional

1. Start by grating the carrots and cucumber into a salad bowl, and then add the beansprouts and scallion/spring onion if using.
2. Now pour in the lime juice and sprinkle on the salt and pepper. Garnish with finely chopped cilantro/coriander leaves ◆

Vegetable pilao

This is a lovely, golden, dry fragrant pilao and is best made with Basmati rice. Basmati is the most famous of the long-grained *indica* type of rice, native to the Indian subcontinent. The other main variety, *japonica*, is the sticky rice favored in East Asian cooking. Both these types belong to the main species, *oryza sativa*. This makes a light meal on its own as well as a good accompaniment to other dishes.

Vegan

Serves 2-3

PREPARATION

5

MINUTES

INGREDIENTS

- 1/2 pound / 225 g rice
- 1 potato, cut into small chunks
- 1 onion, finely chopped
- 2 cloves garlic, crushed
- 1 carrot, finely sliced
- 1/2 cup / 60 g frozen peas or sweetcorn
- 1/2 teaspoon turmeric
- 1/2 teaspoon ground cumin
- 1/2 teaspoon ground coriander
- 1/2 teaspoon chili powder
- oil
- salt

1. Set the rice to cook in boiling water. After 2 minutes, add the potato chunks and continue to cook together for a further 8-10 minutes, or until they are both just done. Remove from the heat and drain.
2. Meanwhile, heat the oil and sauté the onion for 5 minutes until it is becoming soft. Then add the garlic and spices. Cook for 3 minutes.
3. Now add the carrots and peas and stir everything together, cooking for a couple of minutes.
4. Transfer the vegetable mix to the rice and potatoes pan. Combine all the ingredients, using a fork instead of a spoon to prevent the rice from breaking up.
5. Now cover the pan and cook gently for 10 minutes, stirring to prevent sticking ◆

Savory rice with nuts and dried fruit

Vegan

Serves 2-4

PREPARATION 5 MINUTES

15 COOKING

In many cultures rice symbolizes fecundity and good fortune. In some Hindu marriage ceremonies, the couple stand in a shallow basket and have rice showered on their heads as a blessing. In this recipe, pistachios, walnuts or brazil nuts could also be used. The nuts can be left whole or coarsely chopped.

INGREDIENTS

- ½ pound / 225 g rice
- 1 cup / 100 g raisins or sultanas
- ½ cup / 60 g cashew nuts
- ½ cup / 60 g almonds
- 1 stick cinnamon or ½ teaspoon ground cinnamon
- 3 cloves
- 4 green cardamoms
- 1 tablespoon margarine
- ½ teaspoon sugar +
- pinch of salt

+ optional

1. Put the rice into a pan and pour over enough boiling water to cover. Boil for 10-15 minutes or according to packet instructions, until the rice is just cooked and most of the water absorbed. Drain if necessary.
2. Meanwhile, put the raisins or sultanas and nuts into a small bowl and cover with water. Soak for 5 minutes and then drain.
3. Heat the margarine and sauté the cinnamon, cloves and cardamoms for a minute or so before adding the raisins or sultanas and nuts. Stir and cook for 2 minutes.
4. Tip the spices and raisin/nut mixture into the rice and combine well. Add sugar and/or salt to taste. Heat through gently before serving, stirring so that the rice does not catch ◆

Red pumpkin thoran

SPICED PUMPKIN

The pumpkin used here is the large yellow/red variety. Its seeds are often served as a pleasant and nutritious snack, and can also be made into vegetable oil. If you cannot find pumpkin, you could use carrots and french beans.

Vegan

Serves 2-4

PREPARATION
10
MINUTES

INGREDIENTS

1 pound / 450 g pumpkin, peeled and cut into small pieces
1 teaspoon mustard seeds
1 dried red chili, whole
1/2 teaspoon turmeric
4 curry leaves
2 tablespoons desiccated coconut
oil
salt

1. First boil the pumpkin pieces for 10-15 minutes until soft. Drain.
2. Now heat the oil in a pan and add the mustard seeds, chili, turmeric and curry leaves.
3. When mustard seeds splutter add the pumpkin and stir briefly. Sprinkle the coconut on top before serving ◆

Sweet potatoes

Vegan

Serves 4

PREPARATION 15 MINUTES

15 COOKING

Sweet potatoes, originally from South America, are now grown widely in wet tropical regions and in warm temperate areas such as Spain and parts of the US. Although called 'potato' they are not closely related to the ordinary ones.

INGREDIENTS

4 sweet potatoes, peeled and chopped into small chunks

1/2 teaspoon turmeric

1 teaspoon mustard seeds

6 curry leaves

2 tablespoons desiccated coconut

oil or margarine

salt

1. First, boil the sweet potatoes with the turmeric and salt. When ready, drain.
2. While they are cooking, heat the oil or margarine in a pan and fry mustard seeds and curry leaves. When the seeds splutter add the sweet potatoes and stir as they cook for 5 minutes.
3. Now add the grated coconut. This dish can also be eaten as a snack ◆

Cucumber pachadi

The intriguingly-named Spirit Cave in Thailand was found to hold remains of cucumbers dating from almost 12,000 ago, but no-one knows for sure where they originated. We do know however that the Ancient Greeks and Romans enjoyed this cool vegetable in salads and relishes much as we do today. This is an attractive, well integrated dish - cool and hot at the same time.

Serves 4-6

INGREDIENTS

- 2 inches / 5 cms cucumber, grated
- 1 cup / 220 ml yogurt
- 1/2-1 green chili, de-seeded and finely chopped
- 1 dried red chili, left whole
- 1 teaspoon mustard seeds
- oil
- salt

1. Mix together the grated cucumber with the green chili and salt.
2. Fry the mustard seeds with the whole red chili in a drop of oil and stir round. When the mustard seeds splutter after a few moments, remove the red chili.
3. Scoop the mustard seeds into the bowl of yogurt and cucumber. Mix well and serve cooled, with rice, pilao, or puris ◆

Thairu chadam

YOGURT RICE

Serves 2

PREPARATION 5 MINUTES

15 COOKING

Curds or yogurt and milk dishes are popular in India and dairy farming has now made the subcontinent self-sufficient in milk powder and butter. India has over 500,000 villages where agriculture is the main occupation. The seasonal weather plays the key role in deciding whether these millions of people will eat well, or find themselves with a poor reward for their labor.

Lakshmi Menon, Mumbai, India

INGREDIENTS

½ cup / 75 g rice
½ cup / 110 ml yogurt
1 teaspoon mustard seeds
2 dried red chilis, left whole
2 curry leaves
oil
salt

1. Start by cooking the rice for 10-15 minutes or until cooked. Drain.
2. Now mix the rice with the yogurt and add salt. Set aside in a serving dish.
3. Meanwhile, heat a little oil in a pan and when hot, add the mustard seeds, chilis and curry leaves. When the mustard seeds splutter, after a minute or so, add the mixture to the rice and yogurt and stir thoroughly. Remove the whole chilis and then serve warm or cold with lime pickle and papadoms ◆

Spicy cauliflower

Over 60 per cent of India's billion people work on the land, but the government aims to reduce this figure to 50 per cent - presumably to encourage workers into other sectors. The subcontinent is officially self-sufficient in most grains - a great achievement. But of course some people can still not afford to purchase the food they need.

Vegan

Serves 4

PREPARATION **10** MINUTES **20** COOKING

INGREDIENTS

1 cauliflower, cut into small pieces
2 teaspoons mustard seeds
1-inch / 2.5-cm fresh ginger, finely chopped or 1 teaspoon ground ginger
1 clove garlic, crushed
1/2 teaspoon turmeric
1 teaspoon ground cumin
1/2 teaspoon paprika
oil
salt and pepper

1. Heat the oil in a wok or pan and fry the mustard seeds until they pop. Then add the ginger, garlic, turmeric and cumin, paprika and seasoning. Mix well and stir-fry for 30 seconds.

2. Now add the cauliflower and stir it round to coat with the flavorings. Add a little water and simmer, covered, for 5-10 minutes or until the florets are tender and most of the liquid has evaporated ◆

Potatoes with mustard

Vegan

Serves 2-4

PREPARATION 5 MINUTES 15 COOKING

In the south of landlocked Nepal lies Lumbini - the birthplace of Gautama Buddha - and there is archeological evidence of an early Buddhist influence in the country, including a famous column and various shrines. Don't be put off by the quantity of mustard powder: the kick is moderated by the oil and blandness of the potatoes. This delicious dish is very quick and simple to prepare.

INGREDIENTS

1 pound / 450 g potatoes, diced

1/2 red chili, de-seeded and finely chopped

1 tablespoon mustard powder

juice of 1 lemon

2 tablespoons oil

salt

1. First, cook the potatoes in boiling water for 10-15 minutes until done.
2. While they are cooking, mix all the other ingredients to make a dressing.
3. Drain the potatoes when cooked and put them into a serving bowl. Pour over the dressing, mix well and serve ◆

Potatoes with yogurt

Serves 2-4

PREPARATION
5
MINUTES
15
COOKING

Pakistan's economy depends heavily on farming, but this has been badly hit in recent years by war, poor weather and regional political turbulence - not to mention the 3 million refugees who have come in from war-torn Afghanistan.

INGREDIENTS

- 4 potatoes, diced
- 2 tomatoes, chopped
- 1 teaspoon cumin seeds
- 1/4 red chili, de-seeded and finely sliced or 1/4 teaspoon chili powder
- 1 cup / 220 ml yogurt
- 2 tablespoons fresh cilantro/ coriander, chopped
- salt

1. First, boil the potatoes for 10 minutes until cooked. Drain.
2. While the potatoes are cooking, heat a pan with no oil and gently toast the cumin seeds for a few minutes, stirring, until they begin to pop.
3. Now put the yogurt into a serving bowl and mix in the toasted cumin seeds, the chili, cilantro/coriander and salt.
4. Then add the potatoes and tomatoes and mix well before serving warm or cold ◆

Fruit stand in Hanoi market, Vietnam.
PHOTO: DARIUSZ KLEMENS

Spiced new potatoes

Tea remains Sri Lanka's main export earner, but smallholders produce rice, sugarcane, and cashew nuts among other goods. Spices and chilis are also grown. These potatoes are deliciously crumbly, dry and lemony.

Vegan
Serves 4

PREPARATION
5
MINUTES

I N G R E D I E N T S

- 1 pound / 450 g small new potatoes
- 1 teaspoon mustard seed
- ½ teaspoon chili powder
- 2 teaspoons ground coriander
- 1 teaspoon turmeric
- 2 tablespoons lemon juice
- 1 tablespoon fresh cilantro/coriander, chopped
- oil
- salt

1. Start by boiling the new potatoes for 10-15 minutes until they are cooked. Drain.
2. While they are cooking, heat the oil in a wok or frying-pan and fry the mustard seed together with the potatoes. Stir as they cook for 5 minutes.
3. Now sprinkle on the chili powder, ground coriander, turmeric, salt and cilantro/coriander. Fry gently for 10 minutes before serving with the lemon juice poured over ◆

Yellow rice

Serves 4-6

PREPARATION
5
MINUTES
20
COOKING

Astrologers may be consulted as to when is the best time to plant rice in Sri Lanka. The rice-growing ritual includes making offerings to the goddess Pattini in the face of drought or pestilence. No wonder the rice tastes good, after all this nurture and care.

INGREDIENTS

1/2 pound / 225 g rice
1 onion, finely chopped
3 cloves
2 cardamoms
1/2 teaspoon turmeric
1 cup / 240 ml coconut milk
oil
salt

1. Boil the rice for 10 minutes or until nearly done; drain.
2. While that is happening, fry the onion in a little oil, in a pan large enough to take the rice. When the onion begins to soften, add the drained rice and stir it round.
3. Pour in the coconut milk and put in the turmeric, cloves, cardamoms and salt. Mix well and then simmer for 5-10 minutes to let the rice finish cooking ◆

Noodles with ginger

Growing crops still provides most people in Thailand with their livelihood, although industry has been the major growth sector in recent years. The country is known as the rice bowl of Asia as it is one of the main exporters of rice, as well as maize and cassava.

Serves 2-3

PREPARATION 5 MINUTES

10 COOKING

INGREDIENTS

- 1/2 pound / 225 g egg noodles
- 1 teaspoon fresh ginger, finely chopped or 1 teaspoon ground ginger
- 3 scallions/spring onions, finely sliced
- 2 tablespoons soy sauce
- 4 tablespoons fresh cilantro/coriander, chopped
- oil
- pepper

1. Cook the noodles according to the instructions on the packet and then drain.
2. While they are cooking, heat the oil in a wok and stir-fry the ginger with the scallions/spring onions for 1 minute. Then add the soy sauce and cilantro/coriander and cook these for a few seconds.
3. Now put in the drained noodles and season with pepper. Mix well and stir-fry for a minute or so before serving ◆

Com chien

POT-ROASTED RICE

Vegan

Serves 4-6

Vietnamese people are adept at cooking rice in many ways. Although this looks very ordinary, it is genuinely different to other methods of cooking plain white rice. The rice doesn't fluff up as much as in other methods of absorption cooking, but gets a nice nutty flavor as a result. It tastes like Chinese restaurant fried rice, and is a good partner for stir-fries. Use long-grain rice, and peanut oil which can withstand high temperatures without burning.

INGREDIENTS

1/2 pound / 225 g rice
3 tablespoons peanut oil
2 1/2 cups / 600 ml hot water
salt

1. Heat the oil in a heavy pan. Add the rice and fry for 5 minutes or so, stirring frequently, until the rice is translucent.
2. Next, pour in the hot water, which will immediately boil. Season with salt to taste. Reduce the heat, cover and simmer for 10-15 minutes, or until all the water has been absorbed but the rice is still moist.
3. Turn off the heat and leave the pot on the hob for a few more minutes before serving ◆

Mashed sweet potatoes

Sweet potatoes are believed to come from the Mexican region, and certainly Columbus recorded the tuber on his first visit to Hispaniola (now Cuba). In Shakespearean England the plant was well known but it never gained the foothold of its less colorful cousin, the potato. The flesh of the sweet potato can be white or yellow/orange - the latter makes an attractive dish.

Serves 2-4

PREPARATION
10
MINUTES
20
COOKING

INGREDIENTS

1 pound / 450 g sweet potatoes, peeled and chopped
1/2 teaspoon nutmeg
a little milk
1/2 tablespoon margarine
salt

1 Boil the sweet potatoes for 10-15 minutes until soft. Drain and return to the pan.

2 Add the margarine and milk and mash well until smooth. Put in salt to taste and sprinkle on the nutmeg. Serve hot ◆

Papas chorreadas

CHEESE POTATOES

Serves 4

PREPARATION
10
MINUTES

15
COOKING

Potatoes first grew in the Andes, and they were cultivated by the Incas around 4,500 years ago, and this dish is a Colombian favorite. It makes an enjoyably rich side dish, or a filling snack.

INGREDIENTS

4 potatoes, halved or cut into thick slices
1 onion, finely chopped
3 tomatoes, chopped
2 cups / 225 g Monterey Jack or cheddar cheese, grated
2 tablespoons yogurt or cream
oil
salt and pepper

1. First, boil the potatoes until tender. Drain and keep warm.
2. Meanwhile, heat the oil in a pan and sauté the onion for 5 minutes. Then put in the tomatoes and seasoning. Stir.
3. Remove from the heat, cool a little and then pour in the yogurt or cream to make a smooth mixture. Add the cheese and cook gently (especially if using yogurt) until it melts. Pour over the warm potatoes and serve ◆

Vegetable salad

You can serve the salad when the beans and corn are still warm from cooking - they absorb the dressing better.

Vegan

Serves 4

PREPARATION **10** MINUTES

15 COOKING

INGREDIENTS

1/2 pound / 225 g green beans
1/2 cup / 75 g sweetcorn
2 tomatoes, chopped
a few lettuce leaves, torn into small pieces
2 scallions/spring onions, chopped
1 tablespoon fresh parsley, chopped
1 clove garlic, crushed
juice of 1/2 lemon
oil
salt and pepper

1. If using fresh or frozen beans or sweetcorn, cook them in boiling water and then drain.
2. In a salad bowl, mix the beans with the sweetcorn.
3. Next, combine the garlic and lemon juice together with the oil; season. Pour the dressing over the beans and corn and mix well.
4. Now add the tomatoes, lettuce, scallions/spring onions and parsley, and toss before serving ◆

Cariucho

POTATOES WITH PEANUT BUTTER

Serves 2-4

PREPARATION 10 MINUTES

20 COOKING

Like so many of our familiar foods today, the peanut or groundnut came originally from South America. Rather than a true nut, it is a legume and grows underground. Its oils and protein are very nutritious.

INGREDIENTS

- 1 pound / 450 g potatoes, cut into chunks
- 1 tablespoon peanut butter
- 1 onion, finely chopped
- 1 cup / 220 ml cream or yogurt
- oil
- salt

1 Pour boiling water over the potatoes, bring back to the boil and simmer for 10 minutes or until cooked. Drain and keep warm.

2 Meanwhile sauté the onion in the oil, and then stir in the peanut butter. Mix well.

3 Now pour in the cream or yogurt and salt, and cook at a low simmer for 5 minutes, stirring frequently. When ready, pour the sauce over the hot potatoes and serve with salad ◆

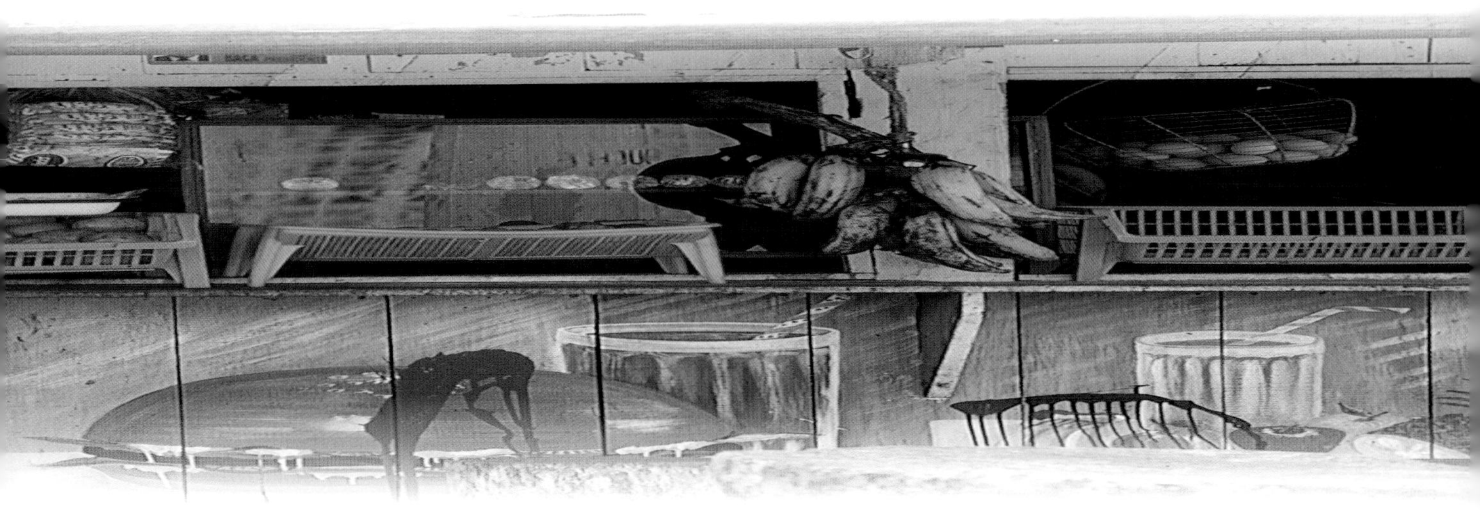

Chirmol

TOMATO RELISH

A traditional Honduran salsa to add flavor and spice to a main dish. It is traditionally served here in Honduras with *frijoles* and *arroz* (beans and rice).

Andrew Pinney, Tegucigalpa, Honduras

Vegan

Serves 2-4

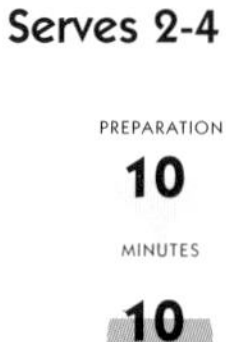

PREPARATION **10** MINUTES **10** COOKING

INGREDIENTS

4 tomatoes, finely chopped
1 onion, finely sliced
3 green or red bell peppers, finely chopped
juice of 2 lemons
¼ teaspoon cumin
1 tablespoon fresh cilantro/coriander, chopped
salt and pepper

1. Place the tomatoes, onion and bell peppers in a bowl.
2. Mix together the lemon juice with the cumin and cilantro/coriander and seasoning, and dress the vegetables with it. If there is time, refrigerate before eating ◆

Rice and tomatoes

Serves 4

PREPARATION
10
MINUTES

15
COOKING

Rice as we know it probably first arrived in the region in the 16th century, possibly brought by the Portuguese from Southeast Asia. But there are wild relatives in the Americas which suggest a common ancestor existed in the Gondwanaland continents before they drifted apart.

INGREDIENTS

1/2 pound / 225 g rice
4 tomatoes, chopped
1/2 cup / 60 g peas
1 onion, finely chopped
1 clove garlic, crushed
1/4 teaspoon chili powder
oil
salt

1. Start by boiling the rice for 10 minutes or according to packet instructions. Drain and return to the saucepan.
2. While the rice is cooking, gently fry the onion in the oil for 5 minutes. Then add the garlic and chili powder and continue to cook for 2 minutes.
3. Now put in the tomatoes and peas, adding salt to taste. Mix everything well and cook for 2 minutes.
4. After that, transfer the tomato and pea mixture into the pan containing the rice and cook together for 5-10 minutes before serving ◆

Corn cakes

Corn cakes turn up in South and Central America as well as parts of the Caribbean. They feature in African cookery too, where maize/corn is also a staple food.

Makes 4

PREPARATION 15 MINUTES

30 COOKING

INGREDIENTS

- 1/2 cup / 75 g cornmeal
- 3/4 cup / 60 g flour
- 2 teaspoons baking powder
- 1/2 cup / 100 g sugar
- 1/2 pound / 120 g margarine
- 2 eggs, beaten
- 1/2 cup / 120 ml milk
- 1/2 teaspoon cinnamon
- 1/2 teaspoon nutmeg

Heat oven to 350°F/180°C/Gas 4

1. Cream the margarine with the sugar. Then sift in the cornmeal, flour and baking powder, cinnamon and nutmeg. Mix well.
2. Next gradually add the eggs and milk, stirring all the time. The mix is quite wet.
3. Grease a muffin or small cake tray and spoon the mixture into the cake pans. Bake for 20 minutes or until the cakes are golden. Leave to cool in the tin for 5-10 minutes. Serve with main dishes and soups, and also as a snack ◆

Green beans with tomatoes

Vegan

Serves 2-4

PREPARATION 5 MINUTES

10 COOKING

Despite its sorry recent history, Iraq has been one of the richest centers of diversity for foods and cultures alike. Persian and Turkish influences abound, as well as traditional Arabian foods like dates, milk, butter and boiled meats. Armenians and Kurds have also contributed: Armenians especially through their pastry cooking and the Kurds with cheeses and yogurt.

INGREDIENTS

1 pound / 450 g green beans

1 onion, chopped

4-6 tomatoes, chopped

1/2 teaspoon ground cumin

1/2 teaspoon ground coriander

1 tablespoon fresh parsley, chopped

oil

salt and pepper

1. Set the beans to cook in boiling water. Drain when done.
2. Meanwhile, fry the onion in hot oil. When it is soft, add the cumin and coriander and cook for 30 seconds.
3. Now put in the beans and cook over a gentle heat for 5 minutes.
4. When ready, pour in the tomatoes, salt and pepper. Cover and cook for 10 minutes, stirring from time to time, before serving with the parsley scattered on top ◆

Garbanzo/chickpea salad

In parts of the Middle East, as in China and the East, food is set into categories such as 'hot' and 'cold'. So in the following recipe chickpeas, onion, garlic and cilantro/coriander are 'hot', while the lemon and yogurt are 'cold'. Using a red onion gives this salad an attractive pink tone.

Serves 4

PREPARATION
5
MINUTES
0
COOKING

INGREDIENTS

1 cup / 150 g garbanzos/chickpeas
1 onion, chopped
2 cloves garlic, crushed
juice of 1/2 lemon
1 cup / 220 ml yogurt
2 tablespoons fresh cilantro/coriander, chopped
oil
salt and pepper

1. Place the garbanzos/chickpeas in a salad bowl.
2. Mix all the other ingredients, except 1 tablespoon of the cilantro/cilantro, together in a blender and pour over the garbanzos/chickpeas.
3. Scatter the remaining cilantro/coriander over before serving ◆

Tomato and cucumber salad

Vegan
Serves 2-3

PREPARATION
10
MINUTES
15
COOKING

The humble mint plant, easy to grow almost everywhere, is a particular favorite in the kitchens of the Middle East and North Africa. It is used widely as an ingredient in many dishes, as a garnish and also in the delicious mint teas which are popular after meals to aid digestion.

INGREDIENTS

5-inch / 12.5-cm cucumber, diced
4 tomatoes, chopped
1 green or red bell pepper, chopped
2 scallions/spring onions, finely sliced
4 tablespoons fresh parsley, chopped
2 tablespoons fresh mint, chopped
1 tablespoon lemon juice
oil
salt and pepper

1. Place the cucumber, tomatoes, bell pepper, scallions/spring onions, parsley and mint in a salad bowl and combine them well.
2. Now mix the lemon juice, oil, salt and pepper together and pour over the salad ◆

Rice with pine nuts

The area around Aleppo (in Syria) specialises in the use of pine nuts mixed with ground meat and bulgur to make *kibbeh* and *kofta* - popular *mezze* (appetizers or starters). This dish is very simple but the pine or other nuts give it a subtle flavor.

Vegan adaptable

Serves 2-4

PREPARATION **5** MINUTES **15** COOKING

INGREDIENTS

- ½ pound / 225 g rice
- 1 tablespoon pine nuts, cashews or pistachios
- 2 tablespoons margarine or oil
- salt

1. First, boil the rice with a pinch of salt and half a tablespoon of the margarine for 10-15 minutes until just done. Drain.
2. While it is cooking, melt the remaining margarine in a pan and sauté the nuts until they turn golden. Scatter them over the rice before serving ◆

Potatoes with saffron and lemon

Vegan

Serves 2-4

PREPARATION 5 MINUTES

20 COOKING

One story of the origin of the crocus flower, whose stigma when dried become saffron, is that Crocus was the name of a beautiful youth who fell in love with a maiden. The two were inseparable – but the gods tired of watching their embraces and unkindly turned the woman into a yew tree while Crocus became a flowering bulb. Saffron is widely used in Moroccan cooking.

INGREDIENTS

- 1 pound / 450 g potatoes, diced
- 2 cloves garlic, finely chopped
- grated rind and juice of 1/2 lemon
- pinch of saffron strands, soaked in a little water
- 1/2 teaspoon turmeric
- 1 tablespoon fresh parsley, chopped
- oil
- salt and pepper

1. Heat the oil in a saucepan and when hot put in the garlic, lemon rind, saffron and its water, and turmeric. Stir well.
2. Now add the potatoes and mix them with the flavorings. Pour in the lemon juice and season with salt and pepper.
3. Next, add enough water to come about half-way up the potatoes.
4. Put the cover on and bring to the boil. Reduce the heat and then simmer, stirring from time to time, for 15 minutes or until the potatoes are cooked, and most of the liquid has evaporated. Garnish with parsley before serving ◆

Glazed onions with raisins

Vegan

Makes 2-3 servings

PREPARATION 10 MINUTES 20 COOKING

Ras el hanout, used here, is the characteristic spice mix of Morocco. The name means 'head of the shop' and conveys the meaning of the spice-seller's own special blend. This delicious and rich sauce is often served with fish or couscous, but it goes well with many other non-Moroccan dishes as it is like a chutney in some ways. Try it with spicy potatoes (p108) or a plain rice and lentil dish (p 143). If possible, use the large red-purple onions.

INGREDIENTS

- 3 large onions, chopped
- 1-2 teaspoons ras el hanout *
- 2 tablespoons raisins or sultanas
- 1 tablespoon honey or sugar
- 1 tablespoon oil
- salt

* This spice mix often contains up to 50 spices. If you cannot find it, garam masala could be used instead or else put in a pinch of the following: cinnamon, mace, nutmeg, allspice and saffron or turmeric.

1. Place all the ingredients, except the honey or sugar, into a saucepan and pour in enough water just to cover the base of the pan.
2. Put the lid on and cook gently, stirring from time to time, for 15 minutes or until the onions are soft and most of the liquid has been absorbed.
3. Now add the honey or sugar, and cook for a further 5 minutes, stirring all the time to prevent burning. The mixture should caramelize a little ◆

Rice and lentil pilaff

Vegan

Serves 4

PREPARATION **10** MINUTES

20 COOKING

Rice and lentils seem to be key elements in several cultures. This dish is similar to the Indian *khichdi* and the Egyptian street-food *kushuri* which is sometimes bulked up with macaroni to make it even cheaper. This dry, pleasant pilaff, teased up with the zest of lemon, makes a good accompaniment to many dishes.

INGREDIENTS

- 1/2 pound / 225 g red lentils
- 1/2 pound / 225 g rice
- 1 onion, finely chopped
- 1 teaspoon ground cumin
- 1/2 teaspoon ground coriander
- 1 lemon, cut into wedges
- oil
- salt

1. Put the lentils into a small bowl and cover with boiling water. Leave to soak for 10 minutes; drain.
2. In a large pan, pour about 2 1/2 cups/600 ml boiling water over the rice and cook for 5 minutes. Drain the lentils and add them to the pot with the rice. Continue to simmer together, covered, until most of the water has been absorbed.
3. While the lentils and rice are being prepared, heat the oil and sauté the onion for 8-10 minutes. When it is beginning to brown, add the cumin, coriander, salt and pepper and cook together for 3 minutes.
4. Scoop the onion and spice mixture into the pan containing the rice and lentils. Stir well to blend all the ingredients, and continue to cook until the rice and lentils are soft and the water almost completely absorbed. Serve with lemon wedges ◆

Tabbouleh

TOMATO, CUCUMBER AND PARSLEY SALAD WITH BULGUR

The look, colors and consistency of food are considered very important in the Middle East. In this popular salad, the creamy-white bulgur makes a good setting for the dark green herbs and bright red of the tomatoes.

Vegan

Serves 4-6

PREPARATION 10 MINUTES

15 COOKING

INGREDIENTS

1 cup / 150 g bulgur
2 scallions/spring onions, finely chopped
5-inch / 12.5-cm cucumber, finely diced
4 tomatoes, finely chopped
4 tablespoons fresh parsley, finely chopped
3 tablespoons fresh mint, finely chopped
4 tablespoons lemon juice
4 tablespoons oil
salt and pepper

1 Prepare the bulgur according to the packet instructions. When ready, drain, and run under cold water.

2 Now add all the other ingredients except the oil and lemon juice. Mix well.

3 Combine the oil, lemon juice and seasoning. Pour over the salad, turning to distribute the dressing ◆

Desserts and Drinks

Girls eating candyfloss, Bangalore, India.

PHOTO: DARIUSZ KLEMENS

Cinnamon bananas

Côte d'Ivoire's capital was moved from Abidjan to Yamoussoukro, home of former president Houphouët-Boigny. The city is described by the *Rough Guide* as a 'colourless administrative centre with its monstrous Basilica' - a reference to the overblown cathedral built by Houphouët-Boigny, requiring vast sums of money. The new capital lies in the Baoulé country which was settled in the 18th century by refugees from the Asante empire.

Vegan

Serves 2-4

INGREDIENTS

- 4 bananas, peeled
- 4 tablespoons breadcrumbs, oats or crushed cornflakes
- juice of 1 lemon
- cinnamon
- sugar +
- oil

+ optional

1. Cut the bananas in half and then slice each half lengthwise. Pour the lemon juice over them and set aside for 5 minutes.
2. Heat some oil in a wok or pan, and while it is warming, roll each piece of banana in the breadcrumbs/oats/cornflakes.
3. Now quickly fry the bananas and drain them on kitchen paper. Sprinkle on a little cinnamon and sugar, if using, and serve at once ◆

Mango snow

Serves 2-4

PREPARATION
5
MINUTES

0
COOKING

If using canned mango, which is often in syrup, the yogurt will help counter the sweetness. Fresh mangos are more tart.

I N G R E D I E N T S

1 x 14 oz / 400 g can mangos, drained, or 1 large fresh mango, peeled and chopped

3/4 cup / 165 ml yogurt or cream

1/4 teaspoon cinnamon

1. Put the mango into a bowl and mash well, or if using a blender place the fruit in it.
2. Then add the yogurt or cream and mix to a smooth purée. Chill and serve, with cinnamon sprinkled on top ◆

Kesari

SEMOLINA DESSERT

Semolina, made from durum wheat, is a widely-used ingredient in Indian cookery. In Italian cuisine it is made into gnocchi while in the Middle East and North Africa it is transformed into couscous. Ideally this dessert should cool in the fridge before serving.

Makes 15-20 pieces

PREPARATION 5 MINUTES

5 COOKING

INGREDIENTS

- 1 cup / 150 g semolina
- ½ cup / 100 g sugar
- 1 cup / 240 ml milk
- 1 cup / 240 ml water
- 1 tablespoon raisins, chopped
- 1 tablespoon cashew nuts, chopped
- ghee or margarine

1. First of all, fry the raisins and cashews in the ghee or margarine and then set aside.
2. Using the same pan, with a little more ghee or margarine as required, fry the semolina to toast it for a couple of minutes. Set aside.
3. Now boil the water, milk and sugar together. Add the semolina, cashews and raisins slowly while stirring to avoid lumps. Cook for 2-3 minutes until the mixture has thickened.
4. Transfer the semolina to a plate and flatten it out with a spoon. Leave it to cool, and then cut into squares and store in the refrigerator ◆

Dal and jaggery payasam

MUNG BEAN DESSERT

Vegan

Serves 2-4

PREPARATION
5
MINUTES
25
COOKING

Jaggery is an unrefined, dark sugar made from the juice of certain palm trees, or from sugar cane. It is considered to be 'heating' (high energy food) and children are often given lumps of it to nibble on during the winter months. It is usually found in cake form and then is crumbled. If you cannot find it, use ordinary unrefined dark sugar. Mung dal are the split form of mung beans, whose beansprouts are very popular as a salad or stir-fry vegetable.

INGREDIENTS

1 cup / 200 g mung dal
1 cup / 200 g jaggery or unrefined sugar, or to taste
1/2 cup / 120 ml coconut milk
seeds of 2 cardamoms, crushed

1. Cover the mung dal with boiling water for 10 minutes. Then put them in a saucepan, pour fresh boiling water over, and boil for 15-20 minutes or until cooked and most of the water absorbed. Drain if necessary.
2. Now add the jaggery, coconut milk and crushed cardamom seeds and stir to dissolve the sugar. Cook for 1-2 minutes before serving hot or cold ◆

Sweet lassi drink

This is extremely easy to make, and a lovely, cool refreshing drink. A lighter version can be made by substituting water for the milk. You can also flavor it with crushed cardamom seeds, or rosewater.

INGREDIENTS

1 cup / 220 ml yogurt
1 cup / 240 ml milk
2 teaspoons sugar
a few drops vanilla or other flavoring
2-3 almonds, finely chopped

1. Put all the ingredients, except the almonds, into the blender and whizz for a few moments to mix well.
2. Pour into glasses and scatter the chopped almonds on top before serving ◆

Rum punch with fruit juice

Vegan

Serves 4-6

PREPARATION

5

MINUTES

0

COOKING

Much of Bolivia's land is the bleak, treeless and windswept altiplano which lies about 4,000 meters above sea-level. And this is where most Bolivians live - the bitter wind mitigated by the extraordinary clear light. The animals are also striking: llamas, alpacas and vicuñas (all related); chinchillas and red fox. Sugar cane - from which rum is produced - grows in the warmer Santa Cruz area.

INGREDIENTS

1 cup / 240 ml rum or brandy
1 cup / 240 ml pineapple juice
1 cup / 240 ml grapefruit juice
1 banana, sliced
juice of 1 lime or lemon
1 tablespoon honey
1 tablespoon desiccated coconut
crushed ice

1 Put everything except the ice into a blender and whizz until well mixed. Pour over crushed ice ◆

Iced tea

Vegan

Serves 2

PREPARATION
5
MINUTES
0
COOKING

Nutmegs were first planted in Grenada in the 1840s, after much shenanigans and stealth by the French and British to smuggle the valuable spice from the Dutch-held Molucca islands (now part of Indonesia). And after that bit of history, how about a refreshing cup of iced tea - flavored with nutmeg of course.

INGREDIENTS

2 teaspoons tea or 2 teabags
2 slices lime or lemon
1/4 teaspoon nutmeg
2 sprigs of fresh mint
crushed ice

1. Make the tea in a pot as usual. Leave to draw for 2 minutes.
2. Prepare glasses by half-filling with crushed ice, and then pour the tea over the ice.
3. Place the slices of lime or lemon on top and sprinkle with nutmeg and mint ◆

Papaya stall, Dominican Republic.
PHOTO: N. DURRELL MCKENNA / HUTCHISON

Rice with nuts and raisins

The first settlers in the islands of the Caribbean were indians from the South American mainland: Arawaks who were cultivators, growing cassava, chilis, yams, potatoes and maize/corn, and Caribs who were hunters. Both groups were devastated by the waves of Europeans with their hunger for gold and spices. In this recipe, using molasses sugar or demerara gives the best flavor.

Vegan

Serves 4

PREPARATION 5 MINUTES

20 COOKING

INGREDIENTS

- ½ pound / 225 g rice
- 6 brazil nuts, chopped
- 1 tablespoon sultanas or raisins
- ½-1 teaspoon sugar
- 1 tablespoon margarine
- 2 tablespoons desiccated coconut

1. Pour boiling water over the rice, add 1 tablespoon of the coconut, and cook for 10-15 minutes until ready. Drain.
2. Melt the margarine in a pan large enough to hold the rice, and sauté the nuts for 1-2 minutes with the raisins or sultanas, the sugar and the remaining tablespoon of coconut.
3. When ready, add the drained rice and mix well before serving ◆

Rum punch

Vegan
Serves 2

PREPARATION
5
MINUTES
0
COOKING

In the post-Soviet era, Fidel Castro's Cuba has become a living museum - sparking a new surge of interest for tourists curious to see communism at work in a warm, friendly country with plenty of rum, dance and music. Grenadine, originally made from the juice of pomegranates, comes in an alcoholic and a non-alcoholic form, but both are red and syrupy.

INGREDIENTS

1/2 cup / 120 ml rum
1 cup / 240 ml pineapple juice
juice of 1 lime or lemon
1 teaspoon sugar
1 teaspoon grenadine +
ice

+ optional

1 Put everything into a blender and pour into glasses with the ice. If liked, you can crush the ice first ◆

Peanut cookies

Christopher Columbus arrived on this Caribbean island in 1493 and named it after the Virgin of Guadelupe in Spain. But its first inhabitants, Carib indians, called it Karukera - 'the island of beautiful waters'. These cookies are simple to make and have a good flavor.

Makes 12

PREPARATION **10** MINUTES **30** COOKING

INGREDIENTS

- 1 cup / 125 g ground peanuts
- 2 egg whites
- 1/4 cup / 50 g sugar
- 1/4-1/2 teaspoon vanilla essence

Heat oven to 325°F/160°C/Gas 3

1. Whisk the egg whites until stiff.
2. Add the sugar a little at a time, beating as you do so. Then add the ground peanuts and vanilla essence, and mix.
3. Grease a baking sheet and drop tablespoons of the mixture onto it, leaving a space between each macaroon so they remain separate.
4. Bake for 20-30 minutes until firm ◆

Bananas with mango

Vegan

Serves 2-4

PREPARATION

5

MINUTES

10

COOKING

'Down in Demerara' goes the chorus of a song, and Demerara - both a county and a river - is in Guyana, South America. And since the name is given to a type of sugar, it is not hard to imagine what is the main export crop here. Demerara sugar is the best for this dessert if you have it. The rum can be omitted of course, but it may be missed. Vegans should omit the yogurt in step 3 below.

INGREDIENTS

- 4 bananas, peeled
- 1 x 14 oz / 400 g can, drained, or 1 large fresh mango, peeled and sliced
- juice of 1 lime or lemon
- 1-2 tablespoons rum
- 1 teaspoon sugar
- 1/2 teaspoon cinnamon

Heat oven to 400°F/200°C/Gas 6

1. Slice the bananas lengthwise and place them in an oven-proof serving dish.
2. Arrange the slices of mango on top of the bananas. Pour over the lime or lemon juice and rum and sprinkle on the sugar and cinnamon.
3. Bake for 10 minutes and serve with yogurt ◆

Coconut and pineapple dessert

Hurricane Mitch swept through Honduras in 1998 leaving behind chaos and destruction. As Honduras is one of the most heavily-indebted countries in the world, the disaster was almost a mortal blow. Many lives were lost, food crops were destroyed and the main export-earners - bananas and coffee - were ruined.

Vegan

Serves 2-4

PREPARATION **10** MINUTES **15** COOKING

INGREDIENTS

1 cup / 75 g desiccated coconut

1 cup / 100 g fresh or canned * pineapple, cut into chunks

1/2 cup / 60 g chopped mixed nuts

1/2 cup / 50 g brown sugar

1/4 teaspoon cinnamon

2 tablespoons margarine

* If using canned pineapple in juice, keep some of the juice for step 3 below.

1 First, put the coconut into a bowl and pour hot water over. Set aside for 10 minutes and then drain.

2 Meanwhile, melt the margarine in a pan and when it is hot put in the pineapple chunks and the sugar. Stir well, and then add the cinnamon.

3 Now put in the drained coconut and stir it in well to mix all the ingredients. You can add some retained pineapple juice if desired. Cook gently for 10 minutes to heat through. Scatter the nuts on top before serving ◆

Avocado dessert

Vegan

Serves 2

PREPARATION
5
MINUTES

0
COOKING

Along with Guadeloupe, Martinique is a French overseas department, and still closely tied to the European country from which it receives a hefty subsidy amounting to 75 per cent of its Gross National Product. Bananas and rum are among its main exports.

INGREDIENTS

1 avocado

1-2 teaspoons sugar

½ teaspoon nutmeg

a few drops kirsch or rum +

+ optional

1. Start by peeling the avocado. Cut the fruit into small cubes and place in two small dessert dishes.
2. Sprinkle on the sugar and nutmeg, and add a few drops of liquor if using ◆

Coconut rice pudding

Venezuela's cooking blends indigenous foods with Spanish introductions - so avocados and maize/corn breads mix with bananas, coconuts and rice. Dishes using coconut in some form, like this recipe, are typical of the coastal region.

Serves 2-4

INGREDIENTS

- 1/2 pound / 225 g rice
- 1/2 cup / 35 g desiccated coconut
- 1 cup / 240 ml milk
- 1/2 cup / 100 g sugar
- 1/2 teaspoon cinnamon
- grated rind of 1/2 lemon

1. Put the rice into a pan and cover with boiling water. Cook for 10 minutes or until the rice is almost ready; drain.
2. Now return the rice to the pan and add the dried coconut, the milk, half the cinnamon, and sugar. Mix well.
3. Cook over a gentle heat for 5-10 minutes, stirring frequently, until the rice is completely ready. Sprinkle on the lemon rind and cinnamon before serving ◆

Ayran

YOGURT DRINK

Serves 4-6

PREPARATION
5
MINUTES
0
COOKING

The biblical Promised Land, described as flowing with milk and honey, in more accurate translation flowed with yogurt and honey. Yogurt seems to have first been produced in the Middle East where is it an essential part of the diet. In one recipe it is mixed with bulgur and then fermented to make *kishk*, a food with ancient origins. Forms of yogurt drink appear from Turkey through to India where it is known as *lassi*.

INGREDIENTS

4 cups / 1 liter water
2 cups / 440 ml yogurt
12 almonds
2 teaspoons lemon juice
a few drops rose water or vanilla
sugar or salt

1 Put half the water into a blender with the yogurt, almonds, lemon juice and flavoring. Add the remaining water to make the desired consistency and then serve ◆

Kab el ghzal/Cornes de gazelle

ALMOND CRESCENTS

Makes 15-20

PREPARATION 15 MINUTES

40 COOKING

These little crescent-shaped cakes or 'gazelle horns' are found all over Morocco. They are delicious for breakfast - or at almost any time of day come to think of it - with a cup of coffee or mint tea. Almonds are an integral part of North African and Middle Eastern cooking, as are other nuts.

INGREDIENTS

- 1/2 pound / 225 g almonds, ground
- 1/4 pound / 110 g powdered/icing sugar
- 1/4 teaspoon ground cinnamon
- 1/4-1/2 teaspoon almond essence
- 4-6 tablespoons rose or orange blossom water *
- 1 egg, beaten
- 6 tablespoons sesame seeds

* from Asian stores

Heat oven to 375°F/190°C/Gas 5

1. Put the ground almonds into a bowl and add the sugar, cinnamon, almond essence, and enough rose or orange blossom water to make a paste. Knead well to integrate the ingredients.
2. Take up walnut-sized pieces and roll them between your hands to form cigar shapes which are thicker in the middle than at the ends, and about 2 1/2 inches/5 cms long.
3. Now pour the beaten egg onto a plate or shallow dish, and sprinkle the sesame seeds onto another. Dip the almond shapes into the egg first and then into the sesame seeds to coat it.
4. Lightly grease a baking sheet and lay the cigar shapes on it, forming them into crescents.
5. Bake for 40 minutes or until they are golden, and cool before serving ◆

Souk (market) in old city, Najaf, Iraq.
PHOTO: CAROLINE PENN / IMPACT

Mint tea

This is the customary drink in the country - and often in the past contained wormwood (absinthe) rather than tea with the mint. Its preparation is almost an art as the maker sips and tastes before deciding the brew is ready. It is normally prepared in an elegant silver pot, and poured from height (to let it cool a little) into tall glasses. The sugar is added to the pot and so is hard to avoid, but after a while its minty sweetness becomes a refreshing familiarity. The tea used is green China tea ('gunpowder' tea), not black tea. It can also be served cold.

Vegan
Serves 2-4

PREPARATION
5
MINUTES

0
COOKING

INGREDIENTS

1 teaspoon green tea
2 tablespoons sugar or to taste
2-3 tablespoons fresh mint leaves
boiling water

1 Put the dry ingredients into a warmed teapot and then pour on the boiling water. Leave to infuse for 5 minutes and then serve ◆

Sweet couscous

Vegan adaptable
Serves 4

PREPARATION
10
MINUTES
30
COOKING

'The love of sweetmeats comes from the Faith' - words reportedly uttered by the Prophet Muhammed who himself apparently was partial to sweet things. Whatever the cause, sweets and pastries are an enticing part of the region's cusine, and the combination of nuts, dried fruits and fresh fruits as in this recipe is hard to resist. The dish can be made vegan by using margarine instead of butter.

INGREDIENTS

- 1/2 pound / 225 g couscous
- 1 1/4 cups / 300 ml hot water
- 2 tablespoons butter or margarine, melted
- 12 dates, stoned and chopped
- 12 almonds, whole
- 1 1/2 cups / 110 g mixed nuts, finely chopped
- 2 tablespoons raisins, currants or sultanas
- 1/2 cup / 100 g sugar, or to taste
- juice of 1 orange
- 1 tablespoon powdered/icing sugar
- 1 teaspoon ground cinnamon

1. To begin, place the couscous in a bowl and pour in the hot water, stirring as you do so (or prepare according to packet instructions). Set aside for 10 minutes.
2. While that is happening, combine the nuts (except the whole almonds), dried fruit, sugar and orange juice.
3. Now set the couscous in a couscousier or sieve above a saucepan of boiling water and steam it for 10 minutes. Rub in the melted margarine or butter and then continue to steam for a further 5-10 minutes.
4. When ready to serve, mix the nut and dried fruit mixture into the couscous and turn it out onto a serving dish. Decorate with the whole almonds, and sprinkle on the powdered/icing sugar and cinnamom to serve ◆

Fresh orange dessert

Orange salads seem to be a North African speciality. They can be served with the main dish, and sometimes include carrots or other salad vegetables. Vegans should omit the yogurt or cream serving suggestion.

Vegan

Serves 4

PREPARATION
10
MINUTES

0
COOKING

INGREDIENTS

4 oranges
1 tablespoon dates, finely chopped
1 tablespoon almonds, chopped
2 teaspoons orange blossom water *
1/2 teaspoon cinnamon

* Available from Asian stores

1. Peel the oranges, also removing the white pith. Slice into circles and arrange on a flat plate.
2. Scatter the dates and almonds over the orange slices and sprinkle the orange blossom water over, followed by the cinnamon.
3. Chill until required, and serve with yogurt or cream ◆

Glossary of food and spice items

Fruit on stall,
Sri Lanka.

PHOTO: ROGER PERRY / IMPACT

GLOSSARY

Allspice
Named because it combines the flavor of several spices (cinnamon, cloves and nutmeg), allspice comes from the dried unripe berries of a small evergreen tree belonging to the myrtle family and native to tropical America. Most allspice is grown in Jamaica.

Asafoetida
Also known as *heeng*, this is a reddish dried gum resin with a strong smell and a garlicky flavor. It also aids digestion.

Bananas/plantains
Bananas probably evolved in south-east Asia and were taken to Madagascar and thence to Africa and the Americas. Varieties range from the red and yellow-skinned dessert types to the big green savory bananas or plantains, a staple in much of Africa and the Caribbean.

Beans, pulses and legumes
Black beans, broad beans, haricot, lima or butter beans, pink, pinto, and red kidney beans originated in South America. Lentils are from the Mediterranean; black-eyed beans/cowpeas from Africa; pigeon peas from Africa or India; soybeans and adukis from China; chickpeas (garbanzos) and mung beans (green gram) from India and *ful medames* or brown beans from Egypt.

In India, 'gram' is the word used by English-speaking Indians for garbanzos/ chickpeas and some whole lentils. 'Dal' is the word for legumes or pulses (seeds) that are split into halves and hulled to remove the skins. So the green mung bean becomes yellow *mung dal* when it is skinned and split.

Beancurd see **Tofu**

Berberé
A paste made from chilis and a blend of spices that is the essential flavoring ingredient in Ethiopian cuisine.

Bulgur and cracked wheat
These are similar, both coming from wheat grains and both being very nutritious, but they are not the same. Both are staples in the Middle East. Bulgur is wheat that has been steamed and then dried before grinding whereas cracked wheat is uncooked wheat which has been dried and then cracked apart.

Cassava/manioc
Of South American origin, cassava/manioc is now cultivated in many tropical regions and from it we also get tapioca. Although it is starchy and low in protein, it is easy to grow and may be left in the ground after reaching maturity without spoiling. It should be boiled before eating as it contains toxins.

Cashew nuts
These grew originally in tropical America and were transplanted in Asia and Africa by the Portuguese and Spanish. The nuts grow on trees and make a curious sight as they hang from the bottom of the cashew 'apple'. After picking the nuts are roasted and then shelled by hand, a tedious process made worse as the shells contain an irritant. Kerala state in India, Mozambique and Tanzania are the main producers.

Cardamom
Cardamoms are the dried fruits of a herb related to the ginger family found in India and Sri Lanka. The spice is usually sold in pods which contain clusters of seeds. Cardamom's sweet pungency makes it popular for flavoring curries and desserts.

Cayenne pepper
This comes from two varieties of powdered dried chilis, and its name derives from a Brazilian Tupi Indian word *quiynha*.

Chilis and peppers
The Americas' most important contribution to the world's spices, chili peppers, together with cayenne, tabasco, paprika and sweet or bell peppers all come from the pod-like berry of various species of *capsicum*. Their spicy hotness arises from *capsaican* occurring in varying degrees in the different types.

Cilantro/coriander
The leaves and seeds of this plant are widely used in the Middle East (where it originated), Mexico, parts of Africa and Asia. The leaves resemble flat parsley and impart a strong flavor, while the seeds are mild and aromatic.

Cinnamon
Cinnamon, used in curry powder and to flavor desserts, comes from the peeled bark of an evergreen tree native to Sri Lanka. For the best flavor, buy it in its curled stick form. Cassia is often sold as cinnamon; it comes from Vietnam and has a stronger flavor.

Cloves
Cloves are the dried flowerbuds of an Indonesian evergreen. Their export was a Dutch monopoly until plants were smuggled out in the 18th century, when Zanzibar and Pemba islands off East Africa became the leading producers. They are used to flavor meats and desserts, and in Indonesia to give aroma to cigarettes.

Coconut and coconut milk
Originating in Southeast Asia, coconut palms provide leaves for roofing; coir (outer husk of the coconut) for matting; copra (the dried white flesh) used for cooking oil, soap, margarine and animal feed; the trees also give timber and shade; the

coconuts give food, drink and alcoholic 'toddy'.

Corn/maize
The Americas' cereal contribution to the world's food supply, today corn/maize is grown widely in Africa and Asia as well.

Cumin
Cumin or *jeera* is native to the eastern Mediterranean, but it has been cultivated also for a long time in India and China. It comes from the dried fruit of a plant related to the parsley family. Either the whole seeds or the ground spice is used.

Curry leaves
The Tamil word for seasoned sauce is 'kari' from which we get 'curry'. Curry leaves, from India and Sri Lanka, look like small bay leaves and when crushed release a curry fragrance. In the West usually only the dried leaves are found. Indonesian bay leaves, *daun salaam* can be substituted, or use curry powder instead.

Curry powder
A combination of spices which should be cooked in a little oil to bring out the full flavor, curry powder usually includes turmeric, coriander seeds, black peppercorns, cloves, cumin seeds, cardamom, nutmeg, mace, cinnamon, ginger, chilis or cayenne powder, fenugreek, garlic, and mustard oil. Try mixing your own.

Dill
Dill comes from the Middle East. Its pungent seeds are used as a pickling spice and for flavoring some Indian dishes. The milder feathery leaves are also used for aroma and decoration.

Fennel
Originating in southern Europe, fennel resembles dill in appearance. Its licorice-flavored seeds are an important spice, while the more delicately flavored leaves are used as a herb.

Garam masala
A mix of spices ground to produce an aromatic flavoring for Indian foods, garam masala may include black pepper, coriander, cumin, cardamom, nutmeg, cloves and cinnamon. It is aromatic rather than hot.

Ginger
The knobbly ginger rhizome comes from Southeast Asia and is a popular ingredient there. The fresh 'root' is crunchy and strong in flavor. Dried ginger root and ground ginger do not have the same pungency.

Granadillas see Passion fruit.

Harissa
This is a fiery sauce made from red chilis, popular in North African cuisine.

Ladies' fingers/okra
One of Africa's indigenous vegetables and related to the cotton plant, okra travelled to the West Indies with the slave ships and is widely used now in Caribbean as well as in Indian cookery.

Lemon grass
A lemon-flavored thick-stemmed grass widely used in Southeast Asia, lemon grass is often combined with the flavors of coconut, chili and ginger.

Millet, teff and sorghum
One of the oldest cultivated foods, millet can grow in poor soils with little rainfall making it an invaluable resource in dry areas. Millet and sorghum, a similar crop, are the staple grains for over 400 million people in the world. Teff is grown in Ethiopia.

Miso
A fermented soybean paste used as a seasoning and soup base. 'White' miso is made with the addition of rice while 'red' miso incorporates barley and has a stronger flavor.

Molasses
Molasses is a by-product of sugar-cane refining and comes in differing strengths according to whether it is the first boiling (light), the second (darker) or the third (blackstrap). It is used to sweeten dishes such as Boston baked beans and to pour over pancakes.

Noodles
In Asia these come in a variety that makes pasta shells or spaghetti seem quite ordinary. There are buckwheat *soba*; 'cellophane' or 'shining' noodles made of ground mung or soy beans; noodles made of rice flour, potato flour, and seaweed. Egg noodles, made of wheat flour, are long and thin.

Nutmeg and mace
These are both part of the same fruit of a tree native to the Molucca Islands in Indonesia. Mace is the delicately-flavored red lacy covering encasing the stronger aromatic nutmeg seed. The main producers are Indonesia and Grenada.

Orange blossom water and rose water
These essences made from distilling fresh orange blossoms or rose petals are used widely in the Middle East and India to flavor drinks, pastries and desserts.

Papaya or pawpaw
The pretty papaya tree originated in tropical America and is now found in most tropical regions. The fruits resemble melons, with a cluster of black seeds in the middle.

Passion fruits or granadilla
Passion fruits grow on climbing plants found in South America. The flowers are used as a sedative while the fruits are eaten raw or used in ice-cream and fruit juice.

Peanuts/groundnuts
These protein-rich 'nuts' are really legumes which originated in South America and were taken to West Africa. They are now grown more widely in Africa than the indigenous Bambara groundnut (*njugo* bean) which, unlike peanuts, is not valued as an oilseed.

Pepper
Pepper, whose vines grow wild

on the Malabar coast of south India, has been the most important spice in the world. Today it is mainly grown in Asia, with India the largest exporter. White and black pepper are made from the same peppercorns but treated differently before grinding.

Pine nuts or pignoles
There are two main types of pine nut - the Mediterranean and the Chinese - the former being the more delicately flavored. These are the seeds from the cones of the umbrella-shaped Portuguese or stone pine tree.

Piripiri
The name has come to mean any chili-based sauce served as a condiment, especially with African dishes.

Pistachios
These nuts grow on a small tree found in Central Asia. The green kernels are prized for their decorative color and fragrant flavor. They are eaten salted like peanuts, or incorporated into nougat and ice-cream. Turkey, Iran and the US are major producers.

Ras el Hanout
This is Morocco's key spice mix. The name means 'head of the shop' - so *ras el hanout* is the spice-seller's choice blend. There are many versions, some with 50 aromatics. Most contain saffron, allspice, cardamom, cinnamon, nutmeg, ginger, turmeric and pepper.

Rice
One of the world's oldest cultivated crops, today over 7,000 varieties are grown. It is the staple food that directly feeds most people. It has a lower protein content than other cereals, especially when it is stripped of its bran layer and polished to form white rice.

Saffron
The most expensive spice in the world comes from the dried style of a crocus - it takes 80,000 flowers to yield one pound/ 450g of the spice. The best saffron comes from Spain, Turkey and India, adding delicate fragrance and vivid color to rice dishes. A Mexican variety, *azafran*, comes from safflower - a plant grown for its seeds which are made into oil.

Sea vegetables
These are an important source of minerals such as iodine and B group vitamins. *Agar* and *carrageen* are used as setting agents instead of animal gelatine and seaweeds such as *nori*, *dulse*, *kombu*, *wakame* and *arame* make seasonings or side dishes. Seaweed is an essential ingredient for *dashi*, the stock that is the basis for many Japanese dishes.

Sorghum see **Millet**

Sesame seeds and tahina
Sesame seeds, *simsim* in some countries, are available in health food stores. They are rich in calcium and protein. A staple in Asian cookery, the seeds are often roasted and used as a dipping sauce. In the Middle East the uncooked seeds are turned into a thick paste, *tahina*. The seeds are also used as decoration and in confectionery.

Smen
This major flavoring ingredient in Moroccan cooking is made from clarified butter, herbs and salt. The smen is aged in an earthenware pot until it attains its characteristically powerful aroma.

Soy sauce and Tamari
Made from fermented soybeans and wheat or barley, yeast and salt, the fragrant brown liquid comes as 'light' and 'dark' types. The dark one is enriched with caramel or molasses. Tamari is similar but stronger.

Sweet potatoes
Widely grown in tropical regions, sweet potatoes came from South America - as did the round or 'Irish' potatoes we may be more familiar with. Cook them in the same way: they are delicious baked.

Tahina see **Sesame seeds**

Tannias and Taros
Tannias also known as yautia and 'new' cocoyams come from America while taros (called also eddoes, dasheen or 'old' cocoyam) are from south-east Asia. Popular in tropical regions they are cooked like sweet potatoes.

Tempeh
This is an ancient Indonesian food, usually made from fermented soy beans but also from other beans or grains. Weight for weight it contains as much protein as chicken and is one of the few vegetable products containing vitamin B^{12}.

Teff see **Millet**

Tofu/beancurd
This is soya bean curd made from soy milk. Crushed soy beans produce a milk which is coagulated and then pressed into blocks.

Turmeric
Native to Southeast Asia, turmeric is a rhizome of the ginger family with a musty flavor and yellow coloring effect. It is used in many spicy dishes as well as to color rice, and for this purpose it is a cheaper option than saffron, though the flavors of the two are considerably different.

Vanilla
Vanilla, a popular flavoring for ice-cream and confectionary, comes from the pods of an orchid plant found in the Caribbean and Central America. Madagascar is the main producer.

Yams
These are underground tubers of vine-like plants. The Yellow or Guinea yam and the White yam are the West African types while the Asiatic yam is found in south-east Asia. An American variety is the 'cush-cush' yam. Although starchy, yams contain enough protein to make them a valuable part of the diet.

INDEX BY REGION AND COURSE

V after an entry = Vegan; Va = Vegan adaptable

MIDDLE EAST

Starters

Main courses

Side dishes

Desserts

INGREDIENT INDEX

V after an entry = Vegan; Va = Vegan adaptable

About the New Internationalist

http://www.newint.org

The New Internationalist (NI) is a magazine produced by New Internationalist Publications Ltd, which is wholly owned by the New Internationalist Trust. New Internationalist Publications is a publishing co-operative based in Oxford, UK, with editorial and sales offices in Aotearoa/New Zealand, Australia and Canada.

The New Internationalist was started in 1972, originally with the backing of Oxfam and Christian Aid, but has been fully independent for many years with some 65,000 subscribers worldwide. The NI magazine takes a different theme each month and gives a complete guide to that subjects, be it global economics or health, the environment or education. The NI group also produces a One World Calendar and Almanac, and books such as The A-Z of World Development in addition to work for international organizations including the UN and the Red Cross.

For information contact:

Aotearoa/New Zealand PO Box 4499 Christchurch. e-mail: newint@chch.planet.org.nz
Australia and PNG 28 Austin Street Adelaide 5000 South Australia. e-mail: sandyl@newint.com.au
Canada and US 1011 Bloor Street West Toronto Ontario M6H 1M1. e-mail: nican@web.net
UK 55 Rectory Road Oxford OX4 1BW. e-mail: ni@newint.org

W. BEINART

About the author...
Troth Wells joined the NI in 1972, helping to launch the magazine and build up its subscriber base. She now works on the editorial team as Publications Editor and has produced three food books **The NI Food Book** (1990), **The World in Your Kitchen** (1993), **The Spices of Life** (1996). In addition she is the English-language editor of *The World Guide* produced by the Third World Institute in Uruguay. She has travelled in Central America, Africa and East Asia, and most recently Morocco.

Photo References

28 Mexican beans, *Isabella Tree/Hutchison*; **34/5** Grinding sorghum, Sudan, *Hutchison*; **36** Local produce, Dominican Republic, *M Durrell McKenna/Hutchison*; **38** Pawpaw/papaya, Sâo Paulo market, Brazil, *Susan Cunningham/Panos*; **39** Peanuts, N Britain, Papua New Guinea, *Isabella Tree/Hutchison*; **41** Cardamom, Kerala, India, *Troth Wells/NI*; **42** Central bazaar, Madurai, India, *Horner/Hutchison*; **45** Spice seller, Castries, St Lucia, *Jeremy Horner/Hutchison*; **47** Corobastos market, Bogota, Colombia, *Jeremy Horner/Hutchison*; **48** Tortilla seller, Mexico, *Hutchison*; **51** Food stall, Cairo, Egypt, *Amedeo Vergani*; **54** Local food, Syria, *Angela Silvertop/Hutchison*; **55** Street seller, Cairo, *Liba Taylor/Hutchsion*; **56** Bakery and sweet shop, Jerusalem, *Mark Henley/Impact*; **62** Cooking cassava, DR Congo, *Errington/Hutchison*; **65** Vegetables and chilis, Banjul market, Gambia, *Hutchison*; **67** Chilis in Abidjan market, Côte d'Ivoire, *Sarah Murray/Hutchison*; **72** Fruit stall, Hong Kong, *Mark Henley/Impact*; **75** Fast food, Bangalore, India, *Dariusz Klemens*; **76** Selling lemons, Orissa, India, *Dariusz Klemens*; **78** Winnowing rice, Bangladesh, *Dirk R Frans/ Hutchison*; **82** Floating market, Thailand, *Jeremy Horner/Hutchison*; **86** Shop sign, Panajachel, Guatemala, *Sean Sprague/Panos*; **90** Squashes at the indian market, San Cristobal de las Casas, Mexico, *Isabella Tree/Hutchison*; **92** Corn on the cob, Xochimilco, Mexico, *John Wright/Hutchison*; **94** Bread-making, Egypt, *Liba Taylor/Hutchison*; **98** Chilis, Rabaul market, N Britain, Papua New Guinea, *Isabella Tree/Hutchison*; **100** Yam storage, Ghana, *Timothy Beddow/Hutchison*; **102** Market stallholder, Arusha, Tanzania, *Crispin Hughes/Hutchison*; **104** Child selling 'pok pok' or Cape gooseberries, Madagascar, *Christine Pemberton/Hutchison*; **107** Tomatoes and aubergines on road stall, Ghana, *Sarah Murray/Hutchison*; **109** Sakina market, Arusha, Tanzania, *Crispin Hughes/Hutchison*; **110** Grinding spices, Bangladesh, *Sarah Errington/Hutchison*; **113** Bazaar food, Varanasi, India, *Horner/Hutchison*; **115** Brass cooking pots, Ladakh, India, *Paul Harris*; **119** Fruit market, Kandy, Sri Lanka, *Horner/Hutchison*; **120** Spices, Sikkim, India, *Dariusz Klemens*; **122** Spices on sale, Guadeloupe, *Pablo/Impact*; **126** Vegetable market, Bangkok, Thailand, *Sarah Murray/Hutchison*; **128** Noodles in Inle Lake market, Burma, *Andrew Eames/Hutchison*; **130** Drinking coconut milk, Pará, Brazil, *Nigel Smith/Hutchison*; **132** Stall in Muisne, Ecuador, *Horner/Hutchison*; **134** Tacos for sale, Puebla, Mexico, *Edward Parker/Hutchison*; **136** Corn cakes, Cotopaxi, Colombia, *Jeremy Horner/Hutchison*; **138** Women making bread, Syria, *Alan Kedhane/Impact*; **140** Pickles, Nablus, West Bank, *Toroai*/Hutchison; **142/3** Medina stall, Fès, Morocco, *Troth Wells/NI*; **144** Traditional food, Egypt, *Liba Taylor/Hutchison*; **147** Market trader, Zanzibar, *Sarah Errington/Hutchison*; **148** Cooking outdoors, Pushkar, India *Goycolea/Hutchison*; **150** Drying fruit, Dominican Republic, *Hutchison*; **153** Castries market, St Lucia, *Jeremy Horner/Hutchison*; **155** Home-grown pineapple, Pará, Brazil, *Nigel Smith/Hutchison*; **156** Plantains and bananas, Amapá, Brazil, *Nigel Smith/Hutchison*; **159** Riobamba market, Chimborazo, Ecuador, *Jeremy Horner/Hutchison*; **160** Preparing the family meal, Cotopaxi, Ecuador, *Rhodri Jones/Panos*; **164** Tuareg making mint tea, Algeria, *Andy Johnstone/Impact.*; **166** Spice souk, Fès, Morocco, *Troth Wells/NI.*

Bibliography

see also notes at the end of the Introduction

Food in History Reay Tannahill (Penguin, London 1988)

Queer Gear Caroline Heal and Michael Allsop (Century Hutchinson, London 1986)

The Evolution of Crop Plants Ed N W Simmonds (Longman, Harlow 1986)

The Oxford Book of Food Plants G B Masefield, M Wallis, S G Harrison and B E Nicholson (OUP, London 1973)

The Von Welanetz Guide to Ethnic Ingredients Diana and Paul Von Welanetz (Warner Books, New York 1982)

Culinary Traditions of the Middle East Ed. Sami Zubaida and Richard Trapper (IB Tauris 1994)

Traditional Morocco Cooking Madam Guinaudeau (Serif 1994)

Moroccan Cuisine Paula Wolfert (Grub Street, London 1998)

Food for the Future Ed Patricia Allen (John Wiley 1993)

Against the Grain Marc Lappé and Britt Bailey (Earthscan, London 1999)

Good Food Margaret M Wittenberg (The Crossing Press 1995)

Organizations

Consumers International
24 Highbury Crescent
London N5 1RX
Tel +44 171 226 6663 Fax +44 171 354 0607
e-mail consint@consint.org.uk
http://www.consumersinternational.org

GRAIN
(Genetic Resources Action International)
Secretariat
Girona 25
pral. E-08010 Barcelona, Spain
Tel. +34 3 3011381 Fax +34 3 3011627
e-mail grain@gn.apc.org

RAFI
(Rural Advancement Foundation International)
International Office
Suite 504
71 Bank Street
Ottawa, ONK1P 5N2
http://www.rafi.org e-mail rafi@rafi.org

The Vegetarian Society
Parkdale
Dunham Road
Altrincham, Cheshire WA14 4QG
Tel +44 161 928 0793
Fax +44 161 926 9182
http://www.vegsoc.org

The Vegetarian Resource Group
P O Box 1463 Baltimore, MD 21203
USA
Tel +1 410 366 8343
e-mail: vrg@vrg.org http://www.vrg.org

Greenpeace and **Friends of the Earth**
http://www.greenpeace.org
http://www.foe.org